A Brief Guide to New Testament Interpretation

A Brief Guide to New Testament Interpretation

History, Methods, and Practical Examples

ROY A. HARRISVILLE

Foreword by Roy A. Harrisville III

WIPF & STOCK · Eugene, Oregon

A BRIEF GUIDE TO NEW TESTAMENT INTERPRETATION
History, Methods, and Practical Examples

Copyright © 2022 Roy A. Harrisville. All rights reserved. Except for brief quotations in critical publications or reviews, no part of this book may be reproduced in any manner without prior written permission from the publisher. Write: Permissions, Wipf and Stock Publishers, 199 W. 8th Ave., Suite 3, Eugene, OR 97401.

Wipf & Stock
An Imprint of Wipf and Stock Publishers
199 W. 8th Ave., Suite 3
Eugene, OR 97401

www.wipfandstock.com

PAPERBACK ISBN: 978-1-6667-3511-6
HARDCOVER ISBN: 978-1-6667-9186-0
EBOOK ISBN: 978-1-6667-9187-7

VERSION NUMBER 031522

To my students

Contents

Foreword by Roy A. Harrisville III | xi
Acknowledgements | xiii
Introduction | xv

Part I: Why Exegesis? | 1
    Faith and the Historical Event as Witnessed to in Scripture | 1
    Historical-Critical Method and Public Ministry | 2
    Brief Remarks on Exegesis and the Understanding of Faith | 3
    The Point of Learning the Exegetical Steps | 4
    The Constant | 5
    The Charisma | 5

Part II: A Brief Review of the History of New Testament Interpretation | 7
    History of Interpretation | 7
    Aids to Interpretation | 17
    Aids to Translation | 17
    Transmission of the New Testament Text | 18
    Sources of the New Testament | 19

Part III: Deciding the Condition of the Text ("Lower Criticism") | 21
    The Greek New Testament | 21
    Presuppositions of Textual Criticism | 22
    The Beginnings of Text Reconstruction | 22
    Illustrations | 23
    The Caveat | 26

Part IV: Source Analysis | 27
Definition | 27
Presuppositions of Source Analysis | 27
The Hypotheses | 28
The Priority of Mark | 28
Illustrations | 29
The Hypothesis | 30
Conclusion | 30
The Caveat | 30

Part V: Form Critical Analysis | 32
Presuppositions of Form Criticism | 32
The Task | 33
The Methods | 33
The Laws of Style | 33
Speech Material | 34
Illustration | 39
The Caveat | 40

Part VI: Redaction Analysis | 42
General Comment | 42
Presuppositions of Redaction Criticism | 43
Illustration | 43
The Caveat | 45

Part VII: Lexicography | 46
The Necessity | 46
Lexicography Presuppositions | 46
History | 47
Illustration | 48
The Caveat | 48

Part VIII: Sociological Criticism | 50
Introduction | 50
Presuppositions | 51
The Task | 51
The Methods | 52

The Sources | 52
The Presuppositions of Sociological Criticism | 53
Illustration | 54
Conclusion | 54
The Caveat | 55

Part IX: Rhetorical Criticism | 56
Definition | 56
Presuppositions | 57
Methods | 57
Illustration | 58
The Caveat | 60

Part X: Structural Analysis | 62
Introduction | 62
Presuppositions | 62
The Aim of Structural Analysis | 63
The Implications | 63
The Method | 64
The Benefits | 64
Illustration By Way of the Parables | 65
The Caveat | 66

Part XI: Post-Structuralism Analysis | 67
History | 67
Presuppositions | 67
Illustration | 68
Caveat | 68

Part XII: Reader Response Criticism | 70
Presuppositions | 70
Method | 71
Illustration | 72
Caveat | 73

Part XIII: Feminist Analysis | 75
History | 75
Presuppositions | 76

Method | 77
Illustration | 77
Caveat | 78

Summary
The Preacher's Burden | 80
The Task | 80
Reactions | 81
Toward a Solution | 82

Glossary | 87
Bibliography | 93
Index of Authors | 97
Index of Scritpture | 99

Foreword

A LAWYER ONCE ASKED Jesus how to inherit eternal life. Jesus asked the man what was written in the law. "How do you read it?" Jesus asked (Luke 10:26). The Lord was asking the man about a text that was already ages old. If the question was pertinent then, it is even more so now with the passage of an additional two thousand years. The manner in which Scripture is read, the assumptions one brings to it, whether one considers oneself above or below it, often determines what one gets out of it.

For the veteran preacher or the novice seminary student, this book by a seasoned, faithful exegete with years of experience in studying the history of interpretation will prove to be a precious resource. My father's broad outline of exegetical methodology will enable one to become acquainted not only with the various methods of interpretation but with their strengths and weaknesses as well. From Origen to feminist interpretation, my father takes the reader through the history of how various scholars have read the New Testament. This book is a fine introduction to that history and gives the reader an opportunity to place each method within its own historical context, thus granting the ability to evaluate each method.

Moreover, my father treats the reader to his own valuable evaluations of each method. At the end of each chapter is a Caveat that brilliantly describes the positive and negative aspects of each method. The author does not render judgements, but he will practice on each method what each method practices on Scripture!

In doing so he provides the uninitiated and the veteran with an invaluable resource that warns against using any one method as a major crutch in exegesis.

Interpretation is a science that requires studied attention to detail, context, authorial intent, etc., but it also requires something more artful. That aspect of interpretation is the purview of the Holy Spirit and demands from the reader not just a bloodless interest in an ancient text, but an actual engagement with it, a dialogue, or as my father insists, a companionship. Rather than thinking of the Bible as a dead letter, one should embrace it as an old friend and enter into a relationship with it in the understanding that the medium of Scripture is never to be divorced from the message. For Christians, that message is Jesus, the crucified Lord. Remove that heartbeat and the text dies, no matter what interpretational methodology is used. Listen to that heartbeat and whatever method is employed and the text will come alive.

So, read. Read with the understanding that the ancients did not live as we do and therefore dive into the words of the past and the methodologies that are vital for us to understand the Bible in the present. This volume skillfully equips the reader with a fresh and insightful introduction to do just that.

Roy A. Harrisville III

Acknowledgements

THANKS TO MY DAUGHTER, Dr. Randi Lundell, for encouraging me to write this little book. She also served as my secretary, proofreader, and editor through the writing process.

Roy A. Harrisville
St. Paul, Minnesota
2021

Introduction

This handbook is designed to introduce the reader to the various approaches to the interpretation of the New Testament. It includes the traditional methods as well as contemporary approaches that have fallen out of love for method. Several of the analyses listed here may have been challenged in contemporary scholarship. However, since the historical question will not down, they need to be reckoned with. The study progresses from the so-called "lower criticism," dealing with the condition of the New Testament text, to the "higher criticism," involved in the actual process of interpretation. The expectation is not that the user, either in sermon preparation or in preparation for lecture, should execute each step or approach, any one of which may be opted for selection. Virtually none of the schools responsible for introducing a given approach dealt with any other than the one of his or her own devising. This study is thus more in the nature of a historical report than an advocacy for a particular analysis.

There is, however, one assumption or point of view underlying the study, and that is that the New Testament text enjoys a carnality or fleshliness, which not merely links it to other ancient literature but is rooted in recognizable human affairs. Limiting oneself to the "lower criticism," since the "higher" is liable to corrupt the biblical text, as some people of faith propose, does little service to the integrity of the text, which requires attention to a message unblemished by what is secular, worldly, carnal, and thus open to reason and reflection as other literature of its kind.

On the other hand, the so-called carnality or fleshliness of the text does not occur of itself but is mediated by the message. For this reason, the New Testament, without any considerable modification, takes over the Jewish concepts of tradition. This tradition bears a peculiarly dual character: it is kerygmatic but at the same time historical. What belongs to event, what is factual and open to investigation, is mediated by the message, the kerygma. The two cannot be separated. For example, if there were no commitment to the death of Jesus Christ as the salvation of the world, there would be no recitation of the details of his arrest, trial, and death. Event, happening, circumstance, and the proclamation by which it is mediated, are inseparable. Whether or not this commingling—which gives priority to the message—occurs with other ancient religious literature is irrelevant. The point is that where there is no message, there is no event, which means where there is no interpretation, there is no text.

From the outset, the Christian faith knows neither a neutral historical documentation, nor a kerygma or proclamation detached from events. The Christian tradition intends to hold the community to the primal history and thus hinder it from becoming a timeless, non-historical, and mythical experience of redemption. This is amply clear in the confessional formulae, which form the oldest recognizable layer of the New Testament witness. The Gospels and individual chapters in the Epistles can be understood as the interpretation or the commentary on the confessional formulae. The proclamation of the post-Easter community is not to be separated from the suffering and dying of the earthly Jesus. The general content of its confession is the once-for-all and unrepeatable event of his dying and rising.

Event and witness are thus inseparably intertwined. This means that the event is transmitted for the sake of the witness; in fact, it would not exist apart from the witness. Precisely this nature of the text makes research so laborious, renders it prone to error, to a multiplicity of interpretations, as has occurred through the centuries and as will be seen here. But this only indicates the force of the biblical text continually to beget interpretation so long as it

Introduction

is read, thus everlastingly proving its priority over its interpretation, the researcher ever at its beck and call. On the other hand, it is certain that the text will never "escape" interpretion as long as the Gospel of the dying and rising Nazarene is heard and read.

Whether or not this characteristic of the biblical account distinguishes it from all other literature of the ancient world is irrelevant; the point is simply that in the Bible the fact comes by way of the message, and for this reason is liable to—or actually requires—researching and investigating. The problem is that modern scholarship has notoriously attempted to separate the event from the message to the detriment of the one or the other. If the separation involves abandoning the event, the message is reduced to myth, legend. And if (as occurs more frequently) it involves abandoning the message, the result is a reduction to sheer data in contradiction of the intent of the text to evoke a response.

This study begins with the lower criticism and leads through the traditional approaches to the more contemporary, which have fallen out of love with method. In each instance an illustration is added in the hope of furnishing concreteness. To each approach is added a caveat, indicating the problems and perplexities attendant on a given approach. But before leading to acquaintance with the text's humanity, by way of which its divinity intends to intrude, the reader is first introduced to a brief history of the New Testament's interpretation, and to the aids and sources for interpretation as well as the text of the New Testament itself.

PART I

Why Exegesis?

Faith and the Historical Event as Witnessed to in Scripture

FAITH IS REFERRED, THROWN back to the tradition of historical event, is continually harking back to it. This tradition has a dual character: It is kerygma, proclamation, but at the same time historical. The one cannot be divorced from the other. From the outset, Christian faith knew no preaching that was detached from history. This is clear, e.g., from the formulae that comprise the oldest recognizable layer of the New Testament witness (e.g., 1 Cor 15:3–5). In this sense, the Gospels and Epistles can be understood as the interpretation of tradition in the shape of formulae. The proclamation of the post-Easter community cannot be separated from the suffering and dying of the earthly Jesus. Event and witness are inseparably intertwined. Thus, we do historical-grammatical work.

Today preaching, instruction, counseling, etc., constitute a new interpretation of the tradition. They are such, whether or not the etiquette of historical understanding is ignored. But if it is ignored, the result could be disaster. On the other hand, when the historical tools are used in disciplined and responsible fashion, freedom for variation can emerge.

A Brief Guide to New Testament Interpretation

Historical-Critical Method and Public Ministry

It is not in our power to deny the application of historical methods to the exegesis of the biblical books. And it is not a sign of special piety or reverence for the Word of God to omit such work. Of course, it is not every man's affair to proceed in such fashion. A person can read the Bible without it. But whoever carries on an interpretation of Scripture for the sake of public ministry (i.e., ministry in the sense of the *Augsburg Confession*, CA XIV: "Of ecclesiastical order they teach that no one should publicly teach [*publice docere*] in the Church or administer the sacraments, unless he be regularly called [*recte vocatus*]")[1] cannot ignore the historical task.

Historical criticism in our situation and time is the most reliable means we possess of preserving the text of Scripture from arbitrary interpretation and thus of hearing it as it intends to be heard. (e.g., the Jehovah's witnesses and the anarthrous noun in John 1:1. The anarthrous noun, when followed by the copula, is definite according to Colwell's rule).[2] Luther masterfully underscored the significance of linguistic studies and methodological exegesis. *Littera*, for him, was and remained the basis. The way to a faithful understanding of a biblical text thus went through its letters—through the historical, not beyond it. "As dear as the Gospel is to us all, it is so hard for us to come to terms with the languages. God has not allowed His Scriptures to be written in two languages for nothing—the Old Testament in the Hebrew, the New Testament in the Greek.... For us this means that we will not hang onto the Gospel without the languages. The languages are the sheath in which this sword of the Spirit is kept."[3]

---

1. *Augsburg Confession* CA XIV, 46.
2. Colwell, "Definite Rule for the Use of the Article."
3. Luther, "To the Councilmen."

Why Exegesis?

Brief Remarks on Exegesis and the Understanding of Faith

If, to borrow an old phrase of Wilhem Dilthey, Scripture consists of "life expressions in fixed, literary form," and if the Bible is people, then listening to these people is of the essence.[4] This is precisely the historical-critical task: to listen and to ask the questions "what does it say?" and "what does it mean?" Again, if the texts of Scripture transcend mere human expression and in their further proclamation are the living voice of the Gospel, the Word of God, then listening is of the essence.

Now, the distance of years over which dialogue between author and interpreter occurs places the interpreter at a disadvantage. But it is precisely for the sake of telescoping that distance that exegesis is done. The tools are not to be acquired and used for their own sake, as though the determination of the meaning of a word within the history of its usage constituted exegesis. Nor are they to be spurned by the "practical" man as belonging exclusively to the specialist. They are the proper aids to dialogue, requiring to be used to the limit by those who cannot be content with gleaning broken bits of their biblical companions' conversation, but whose calling requires that they hear as much as it is humanly possible to hear.[5]

On the other hand, since that living voice required the response of the total person—mind, heart, and will, the whole self—then they must also, in true Christian faith, give themselves to the text; it requires his/her own surrender to achieve its intention. Once it was asserted that a proper reading consisted in furnishing program notes to the biblical writer's performance. Now it is a truism that apart from presuppositions that prejudice conversation with their text, the reader, preacher, or teacher may legitimately bring all of oneself to its reading. Love of persons requires not merely a beholding but a self-revealing as well, whatever the risks. Thus, Luther knew how to emphasize the significance of an "experiential

---

4. Dilthey, *19 Jahrhundert*, 390.
5. Bultmann, "Problem of Hermeneutics."

understanding." Two days before his death he wrote: "*Virgilium in Buccolicis et Georgicis nemo potest intelligere, nisi fuierit quinque annis Pastor aut Agricola. Ciceronem in Epitolis (sic praecipio) nisi 20 annis sit versatus (employed) in republica aliqua insigni (with something notable). Scripturas sacras sciat se nemo gustasse saitis, nisi centum (!) annis cum Prophetis Ecclesias gubernarit. Wir sind Bettler. Hoc est verus.*"[6] In a masterful way Luther speaks here of his feeling of inadequacy over against the depths of Scripture. But the same Luther underscored just as masterfully the significance of linguistic studies and methodological exegesis. *Littera* is and remains the basis. The way to a religious understanding of a biblical text goes through its letters, not beyond them, for this is the way of the Gospel writers themselves. Otherwise, one's own ideas and experience are made the norm of understanding.

The Point of Learning the Exegetical Steps[7]

Faith is referred to the tradition of the historical event and is continually referred to it. For this reason, the New Testament takes over, without modification, the Jewish concepts of tradition (i.e., *paradosis* and its verbal relatives (1 Cor 11:23; 15:3; 7:10)). This tradition bears a peculiarly dual character: It is kerygmatic but it is at the same time historical tradition. The historical and the kerygmatic components of the tradition cannot be divorced from one another. From the outset, the Christian faith knows no preaching detached from history. The test of exegesis is thus to assess whether the sermon spoken to this concrete situation did justice to the task, missed it, abbreviated it, or weakened it.

---

6. English translation: "No one can understand Virgil in the *Bucolics* and *Georgics* without having spent five years as shepherd or farmer; or *Cicero* in the Letters (as I teach) without having been occupied with something important in the republic for twenty years. So no one can taste Holy Scriptures enough without having ruled with the church prophets for ten years. We are beggars. That is for sure." (Translation by Roy A. Harrisville)

7. Cf. Frör, *Biblische Hermeneutik*, 11–19.

Why Exegesis?

The Constant

Within all the changes and transformations, the situation of the wandering people of God remains the same. They are the same gifts from which it lives, the same temptations and inner conflicts that threaten it. What had encountered it on its way through the centuries and still will encounter it is paradigmatically given in the sermon volume of the Old Testament and New Testament. This contemporaneity throughout all the changes in concrete circumstances makes possible the building of a bridge from the preaching of the text to the preaching of today. The community today can understand what was preached to the community of yesterday because it is addressed by the same Lord and is engaged in the same struggle of faith.

The Charisma

So, the historical work for preacher and catechist is a laborious thing, since I have to contend not only with a preaching text, but also with its history. On the other hand, it can mean freedom: the text loses its compulsion, its legality. It gives me the freedom for variation. Gerhard von Rad (1901–71) has pointed out that this freedom for variation is a charismatic event that can occur but cannot be fixed by methodology.[8] But the interpreter cannot meet the dangers that lurk there for him/her by fearing them and retreating to some more practical method, but only by taking the bit of the Spirit between his/her teeth and allowing himself/herself to be led by Him. Preaching and instruction today is new interpretation of the tradition whether or not the rules of historical understanding are consciously or unconsciously ignored. But in that case, those who are unconscious and uncontrolled can create disaster. So, it is better to use them consciously in order to employ them in obedience. For the freedom for variation can only bear fruit when it is used in obedience, discipline, and responsibility. It goes without saying that the charismatic service of reinterpretation is not done

8. Von Rad, *Old Testament Theology*.

A Brief Guide to New Testament Interpretation

in the solitariness of the private individual, but in conversation with the fathers of the faith and with those brothers and sisters who share it now.

PART II

A Brief Review of the History of New Testament Interpretation

History of Interpretation

Interpretation in Primitive Christianity

IN THIS PERIOD THE Christian community appropriated the Holy Scripture of the Jewish community as its own. This corresponds to the fact that the New Testament cites the Jewish Scripture exclusively as "Scripture,"[1] though the new authority of the "Lord" and the apostles had appeared alongside it. The New Testament authors employed the Old Testament, in some instances without too great attention to their original context and meaning. On the other hand, a method of interpretation was not lacking. In addition to the appropriation of Jewish methods of exegesis,[2] and in addition to citing

---

1. Cf. e.g., John 10:35, "Scripture cannot be annulled"; 1 Cor 15:3, "Christ died for our sins in accordance with the Scriptures"; 1 Pet 1:20–21, "no prophecy of Scripture is a matter of one's own interpretation, because no prophecy ever came by human will, but men and women moved by the Holy Spirit spoke from God." The Word in Heb 2:6 that "someone has testified somewhere," is an allusion to Old Testament Scripture.

2. *Conclusio a minore ad maius* ("from the lesser to the greater"), as in 2

the Old Testament in support of ethical admonitions, to references to Old Testament figures and narratives as types or warnings, there appeared the typological interpretation. According to typological exegesis, specific events and figures of Old Testament history are seen as preparation for the saving events of the eschatological present, and thus are written down for the Christian community. In this way—in contrast to allegory—the historicity of the narrative is not contested, but the eschatological event in Christ and in the church is regarded as the realization of that which occurred in the structural past. In the typological interpretation of the Old Testament, the basic position of primitive Christianity toward the Old Testament is most clearly to be seen. The earliest Christians were ruled by the faith that the present was the last period before the final salvation. Against that background of this belief, the Old Testament appears as God's word, which takes its divine meaning only on the basis of the fulfillment experienced or immediately awaited. Thus, the Old Testament was understood from the very beginning to be a prophecy. The prophetic proof thus fulfilled the description of the life of Jesus. But two things need noting. First, the traditionally interpreted Scripture is not, as it was for the Jews, the sole criterion for thought and life. Rather, the tradition of the life of Jesus and the experience of the community rendered the Old Testament the reference to the eschatological fulfillment. Second, the Christian position toward the Old Testament is from the very beginning a critical one. Jesus claims the authority to give the law

---

Cor 3:10–11 ("for if what was set aside came through glory, much more has the permanent come in glory"); conclusion by analogy as in Mark 2:24–26 ("The Pharisees said to him, 'Look, why are they doing what is not lawful on the sabbath?' And he said to them, 'Have you never read what David did when he and his companions were hungry and in need of food? He entered the house of God, when Abiathar was high priest, and ate the bread of the Presence, which it is not lawful for any but the priests to eat, and he gave some to his companions'"); etymological interpretation as in Matt 3:23 ("There he made his home in a town called Nazareth, so that what had been spoken through the prophets might be fulfilled, 'He will be called a Nazarene'"); *gematria* as in Rev 13:18 ("This calls for wisdom; let anyone with understanding calculate the number of the beast, for it is the number of a person. Its number is six hundred sixty-six"); and allegory.

and the prophets their proper meaning. The Apostle Paul opposes to the "letter," not yet understood by the Jew, the "scriptural meaning" understood by faith. And though in the later New Testament the divine authorship is claimed for Scripture and prophecy as per the Jewish-Hellenistic tradition, the Lord is the final authority, and the Old Testament receives its validity exclusively from the fact that the veil has been lifted "in Christ" (cf. 2 Cor 3:14).

Interpretation in the Ancient Church and Middle Ages

For the beginnings of interpretation in the ancient church and Middle Ages there are only sparse witnesses. They are limited to the Gnostics and other heretics of the second century. An exegesis regulative for the period following was first established in the Alexandrian school. Clement of Alexandria (c. 150–215) wrote his *Hypotyposes*, and Origen (c. 184–253) marked the high point of the ancient church's exegesis. Thus, the exegesis of this period began with the Gnostic heretics, and is the concern of the schools, not of the pulpit. The heretics of the second century were interested in claiming the tradition in their support. Previously, such claims were made by altering the Scripture text itself. In view of the result and conclusion, the fixing of the tradition became a *sine qua non*. Attempts were then made to interpret Scripture so as to prove the interpreter's agreement with this norm. Thus, the *Antitheses* of the Gnostic Marcion of Sinope (c. 85–160) are intimately connected with the establishment of a canon. This type of commentary on the tradition had its prototype in the Hellenistic philosophical schools, which asserted their continuity with their founders by interpreting their writings, considered to be canonical. The result was that there was little or no connection with their Jewish type of exegesis. Where the Old Testament was an object of interpretation, there was no room for the influence of Jewish exegesis.

Origen was the most significant exegete of the old church. He employed the three most important norms of interpretation: *scholia* (explanations of individual passages), commentaries (expositions of entire biblical books), and homilies (doctrinal essays), now sermons. The methods of Origen's exegesis correspond with Hellenistic usage. At the base lay a comprehensive text-critical work. Then, by way of allegory, he proceeded to establish the spiritual sense of Scripture. The importance of this interpretation lay in Origen's theology. He was not concerned with the data witnessed to in Scripture but with the supra-historical, divine truth revealed in it. If the struggles with Gnosticism in the middle of the second century led to the establishment of a Christian interpretation, in the course of the third century there was no genuine thrust toward exegetical work. The Arian controversy revived interest in exegesis, and now became the affair of the bishops. A new center of interpretation arose in Antioch, its tradition initiated by Lucian of Samosata (c. 125–180). Antioch was noted, above all, for its textual criticism, which was uninfluenced by Platonism, as was Alexandria, and which came to be determined by a *heilsgeschichtlich* (salvation-historical) view of the biblical revelation. Allegory was thus rejected as mere speculation. In its place appeared the emphasis on the literal meaning interpreted typologically. Theodor of Mopsuestia (350–428) was Antioch's most important representative. Alongside him was John Chrysostom (347–407), the foremost preacher of the Greek church and the authority for Greek exegesis in the periods following. With the doctrinal struggles of the fifth century, in the course of which the Antiochenes were attacked by Cyril of Alexandria (375–444), a new period of interpretation opened. The trend was now in the direction of the canon; a canon of the exegesis of the church fathers.

In the Greek Middle Ages, exegesis stepped into the background. In the West, the exegetical writings of the ancient fathers were further transmitted. However, Latin exegesis went beyond the fathers in the tradition of Alexandria and Antioch. Ambrose (339–397) was an allegorist; Jerome (342–420) emphasized the grammatical-historical aspect. The commentaries of Augustine (354–430) led further to the problems of the text and were constitutive for later exegesis. His *De Doctrina Christiana* gave the proper guidelines, which were to regulate the exegesis of the entire Middle Ages. In the waning of doctrinal controversies, exegesis

A Brief Review of the History of New Testament Interpretation

was strongly determined by the encyclopedic interests of antiquity. The real thrust now came from monasticism. Exegesis became the affair of the cloister. As a result, exegesis in the early Middle Ages was oriented to the practical concerns of liturgy and preaching. This interest was coupled with a clear predilection for the spiritual meaning of Scripture. In the twelfth century, exegesis came more and more to include the discussion of teleological problems. Systematic theology had begun to declare its independence. This coincided with the development of monasticism in this period, in which the cloister and school created a synthesis. In the period of late scholasticism, exegesis took its shape from the doctrinal lectures in the universities. In this period, also, Aristotelianism (Aristotle, 384–322 BC) began to work its influence. Exegesis involved the meticulous division of the text into hierarchies of importance and search for meaning according to the scheme of the four causes: *causa materialis, causa efficiens, causa formalis,* and *causa finalis.* In order for a house to be built, materials are required: a builder must organize the material according to a plan, the end product must embody the essence of "house," and, finally, no house would be built were there no need for a protective cover. In this way, the question concerning the actual intention of the text became regulative. All the great scholastic theologians were involved in exegesis: Bonaventura (1221–74); Albert the Great (1200–1280); Thomas Aquinas (1225–74). Philological work on Scripture continued. *Catenae* and concordances were created. Late Scholasticism was more or less unfruitful from an exegetical standpoint. All agreed on the supernatural authority of Scripture. The Bible became the criterion in the struggle for church renewal. But there were no theological controversies in the area of exegesis. Further, meditation and popular piety claimed the Scripture. During this stagnation in the late Middle Ages, the humanistic concern with the Bible and its text began, connected at the end of the Middle Ages with the piety inculcated by the Brothers of the Common Life (*Fratres Vitae Communis,* fourteenth century).

A Brief Guide to New Testament Interpretation

Interpretation in Humanism, Reformation, and the Modern Period

First of all, Humanism created the technical and methodological bases for exegesis in the modern period. Text recension and grammatical and textual studies of the biblical languages were the order of the day. Yet interest in the meaning of the biblical text had little to do with the theology of Humanism. Erasmus (1469–1536), for example, allegorized, extracting the spirit of the letter from the verbal.

The Reformation gave to exegesis its dominant position in theology. Martin Luther's (1483–1546) exegesis proceeded *a la* the Middle Ages and was limited to questions of textual criticism and philology. What was completely new, however, was the theological understanding that Luther gained in the course of his Psalms lectures; namely, the distinction between letter and spirit. According to Luther, that exegesis is spiritual, which makes the distinction, but not an exegesis that allows for an allegorical meaning in addition to or beyond the literal sense. The "spiritual," that is, the proper, the hermeneutically true, the Christologically understood literal meaning is the spiritual meaning. The four-fold sense of Scripture (the *sensus literalis* = the literal sense; the *sensus allegoricus* = faith and the teaching of the church; the *sensus moralis* (typological) = Christian activity, morals; the *sensus anagogicus* = hope, the final expectation of God, hence the *littera gesta docet, quid credas allegoria, moralis quid agas, anagogica qui tendas*) is dispensed with once it is recognized that the letter understood Christologically, the letter which history speaks of, always includes the *opus Christi* and thus the *sensus moralis* or *tropologicus*.[3] Luther's view reached maturity in his lectures up to 1519. The problem of exegesis was sharpened when Luther debated with the Fanatics, and with Erasmus and the Swiss Reformers. He maintained the clarity

---

3. The traditional four-fold sense of Scripture are the literal (*sensus literalis*); allegorical (*sensus allegoricus* or *tropologicus*); anagogical (*sensus anagogicus*); and moral (*sensus moralis*). Hence, the literal speaks of deeds, allegory to faith, the moral how to act, and anagogy to our destiny (*littera gesta docet, quid credas allegoria, moralis quid agas, anagogica qui tendas*).

A Brief Review of the History of New Testament Interpretation

of the letter of Scripture, which corresponds to the clarity of the sense. What for Luther contributed to the literal meaning was the determination of the meaning of relations of words and of historical connections. The boundary between exegesis and dogmatics was fluid, as well as the transition to application, but this fact was due to Luther's hermeneutic. The Scripture, he contended, had everywhere but one single *sensus*: Christ. Luther's lectures dealt predominantly with Old Testament texts and dealt with only the Epistles of the New Testament.

Some commentaries were written, set down by Luther's pupils. For a look into Luther's exegesis, it is necessary to consult his exegesis of the Psalms, the Decalogue, the Lord's Prayer, the Magnificat, etc., his sermons and postils, as well as his prefaces to the German Bible. The translation of the Bible played a great role. For this reason, Bible revision assumed a larger place in Lutheranism than anywhere else. What was said of Luther applies, to a degree, also to the other Reformers, though Melanchthon (1497–1560) never completely suppressed humanistic influence. The *Loci* of 1521 intended to be a scientific study of Reformation theology but were bound to rhetorical interests. Rhetorical and dialectical categories flanked the philological and historical explanation of texts. Allegory and analogy were rife in the transition from word to content of Scripture. But since Zwingli (1484–1531) and Oecolampadius (1482–1531) entered the lists against the Wittenbergers on the Lord's supper, the whole debate became exegetical in nature. The Swiss interpreted the Words of Institution figuratively or topically. Calvin's (1509–64) commentaries and sermons embraced, with the exception of Revelation, every book of the Old and New Testaments. He was cautious about the Messianic typology of the Old Testament and permitted it only where the New Testament required it. He confined the historical meaning of the Psalms to David and Solomon, but in his approach to the Psalms, to David and Solomon, metaphors (*tropoi*) and figures were uncovered, as well as erroneous quotations in the New Testament and contradictions in the Synoptic tradition. In contrast to Andreas

Osiander (1498-1552), Calvin's Gospel harmony was limited to the synoptists.

In Lutheranism, exegesis was fixed by the Formula of Concord, on the basis of which it had reached its goal with Flacius (1520-75) and Martin Chemnitz (1522-86), continued by Johann Gerhard (1582-1637). It was formally delineated by a dogmatic-polemic principle, materially by the hermeneutical canon of the analogy of faith. What was left to philological-historical work was used largely for polemics and apologetics. Roman Catholicism made some exegetical headway in the sixteenth century, though it suffered from the Council of Trent's (1545-63) subordinating exegesis to dogmatics.

The period of the confessions was primarily interested in the unfolding and defense of doctrine. Exegesis became the handmaid of dogmatics, its function to deliver the *dicta probantia* (proof texts). Exegetical work began to increase, however, among those hereticized by their various churches. The Dutch Arminians (e.g., Jacobus Arminius [1560-1609], Hugo Grotius [1583-1645], Campegius Vitringa [1669-1722], J. J. Wetstein [1693-1754]) were the first to do exegesis completely independent of dogmatic considerations. As a result of the ecclesiastical mix and political crises in England, Deists undertook criticism of the Scripture in the name of reason and nature. Their criticism directed itself first of all to the Old Testament, since the Puritans had made it the basis for their political and legal structures.

In pietism, exegesis had a practical function. It was independent of dogmatics and made particular use of philology and history. The use of Scripture dominated, however, rather than the understanding of Scripture, with an emphasis on the application rather than the senses. Francois Turretin (1623-87) and J. A. Ernesti (1707-81) emphasized the purely literary treatment of the biblical writings and demanded differentiation between Old and New Testaments. In the eighteenth century, J. S. Semler (1725-91) emphasized the historical character of all religious traditions, including the canon. His maxim read, "free investigation" of the Bible. Historical criticism thus became independent of the miracles

A Brief Review of the History of New Testament Interpretation

of the biblical text. J. D. Michaelis (1717–91) drew other consequences of Semler's view and founded the literary-critical science of the *Introduction to the New Testament* (1750). Still, exegesis was drawn into the struggle between traditionalists and supernaturalists. The theological relevance of the historical-critical method appeared only when reflection on the problem of history overcame the questions concerning reason and revelation, presuming a taste for the question of the relation between history and revelation.

In the nineteenth century, Ferdinand Christian Baur (1792–1860) and his pupils, and later Albrecht Ritschl (1822–89), thought through the implications of the historical character of all theology. The literary-critical concentration in this century benefited from the development of the historical sciences for theology and classical antiquities, historiography, and the study of religions.

At the threshold of the twentieth century, the History of Religions school together with the eschatological interpretation of Albert Schweitzer (1875–1965) claimed the heights. It had overcome the "Life of Jesus" research from H. S. Reimarus (1694–1768) to William Wrede (1859–1906) and was soon supplemented or corrected, first in the Old Testament (Hermann Gunkel, 1862–1932) then in the New Testament (Martin Dibelius, 1883–1947; Ernst Lohmeyer, 1890–1946, et al.) by form-critical, and later by redactions-critical studies. Due to the influence of Karl Barth (1886–1968), from 1919 to 1945 concentration on the "Word" resulted in "theological," that is, practical-dogmatic interpretation of Scripture, often at the expense of historical criticism. Without contesting the value of his concentration, Rudolf Bultmann's (1884–1976) call for existential interpretation combined the problems of exegetical method and hermeneutics.

Reflections

To date, recent interpretation, in terms of historical-critical method, which has had the lion's share in this study, has fallen on bad times. The reason cited for the malaise is that the method has led to a multiplicity of interpretations, leading to confusion or worse, confounding. But in face of the newest approaches, this study insists that whoever carries on an interpretation of Scripture for the sake of public proclamation, in the sense of the Augsburg Confession XIV ("of ecclesiastical order they teach that no one should publicly teach [*publice docere*] in the church or administer the sacraments, unless he be regularly called [*recte vocatus*]")[4] cannot ignore the historical aspects revealed or assumed by the text, no matter to what confusion it may lead. Attention to situation and time, however fraught with error, at least intends to serve the text of Scripture from arbitrary interpretations and thus of hearing it as it intends to be heard.

On the other hand, the understanding of the biblical texts is not confined to the mere facts, but also by the viewpoint of the interpreter, however inchoate and needing discovery. Nor is interpretation reserved for the reader, apart from whatever historical data the text may offer. It is true that the *Sache* (the subject matter) of the text is not subordinate to the historical concern. It is not true that it could just as well be omitted, or that it would be more honest to omit so as to register the mere facts, or, as per contemporary interpretation, to register the response of the reader as somehow "creating" the text. If Scripture intends to be heard as God's call to belief, concentration on the *Sache* of the text is the appropriate concentration.

There is a dualism here: first the critical, then the "dialogical." Both belong to the essence of encounter with the text. The question is how the two relate to each other. First, the canon gives the context. The interpretation of the Old Testament is not possible solely on the basis of its self-understanding, but only in connection with the witness of the New Testament community. Second, no one can omit the whole history of exegesis, beginning at zero. This is the error of sectarians. The dogmas and confessions of the fathers are an exposition of the Scripture, whether as defense against heresy, or whether as pregnant condensation. But since the hermeneutical

---

4. *Augsburg Confession,* CA XIV. "Of ecclesiastical order they teach that no one should publicly teach (*publice docere*) in the church or administer the sacraments unless they be regularly called (*recte vocatus*)."

A Brief Review of the History of New Testament Interpretation

process never comes to a final conclusion, exegesis can never elect for an interpretation laid down for all time. The voices of the fathers and others are helpful conversation partners. Finally, the interpretation of texts in the oral word in the assembled community is the real, appropriate use of Scripture. Every other use in its variegated forms can only be understood as originating in leading back to the oral word heard in the assembled community.

Aids to Interpretation

The manual edition of the New Testament is the *Novum Testamentum Graece*, edited by Eberhard Nestle, Barbara and Kurt Aland, twenty-eighth edition. For exegetical work on the first three Gospels, a synopsis is indispensable (*Synopsis Quattuor Evangeliorum*, ed. Kurt Aland).[5] Since the apparatus of the synopsis is insufficient, reference to the Nestle text is required.[6] Further, since the authors of the New Testament often refer to the Old Testament, they do so most often to the *Septuagint* (LXX). The accepted edition is Alfred Rahl's *Septuaginta*.[7] Equally important is knowledge of the texts of the Jewish sect of Qumran by the Dead Sea. Frequently, work on the New Testament requires attention to later Christian sources, such as the writings of the so-called Apostolic Fathers.

Aids to Translation

The modern lexicon for the total area of Greek language is Liddell-Scott's, *A Greek-English Lexicon*.[8] For work on the New Testament, Bauer-Arndt-Gingrich-Danker is indispensable.[9] The *Theological*

---

5. Nestle-Aland, *Novum Testamentum Graece*.
6. Nestle-Aland, *Novum Testamentum Graece*.
7. Rahlfs-Hanhart, *Septuaginta: id est Vetus Testamentum Graece iuxta LXX interpretes*.
8. Liddell-Scott, *Greek-English Lexicon*.
9. Bauer, Arndt, Gingrich, and Danker, *Greek-English Lexicon*.

A Brief Guide to New Testament Interpretation

Dictionary of the New Testament, edited by Gerhard Kittel,[10] is not a lexicon in the true sense but a collection of monographs on theologically important New Testament concepts. A necessary aid for translation and exegesis of difficult passages is Blass-Debrunner's *Grammar of New Testament Greek.*[11] Finally, one can often get a survey of the appearance and usage of words in the New Testament with the aid of a concordance. Moulton-Geden's *A Concordance to the Greek Testament*[12] is complete, though it uses the text of B. F. Westcott and F. J. A. Hort.[13]

Transmission of the New Testament Text

There are a great number of manuscript witnesses to the New Testament. Their arrangement and evaluation, which aim at offering the original text wherever possible, is the task of textual criticism. This goal, however, can only be approximated, thus the search for the oldest manuscript tradition, and for the allegedly "best" text form. The humanist Erasmus of Rotterdam produced the first printed Greek New Testament in 1516. It was based on poor manuscript witnesses and hastily constructed. The *Complutensian Polyglot,* readied in 1514 and published in 1520, was an improvement. These editions, well into the eighteenth century, were the *textus receptus,* or official texts in use.

The first critical editions, offering several readings on individual passages, originate with the Tübingen scholars Johann Albrecht Bengel (1687–1752) and Johan Jakob Wettstein (1693–1754). Modern text criticism began in the nineteenth century, reflected in the editions of Constantin von Tischendorff's (1815–74) *Editio Octava Critica Maior,*[14] appearing in 1869/1872, and those

---

10. Kittel, Bromiley, and Gerhard, *Theological Dictionary.*
11. Blass, DeBrunner, and Funk, *Greek Grammar of the New Testament.*
12. Moulton and Geden, *Concordance to the Greek Testament.*
13. Westcott and Hort, *Greek New Testament.*
14. Tischendorf, *Novum Testamentum.*

A Brief Review of the History of New Testament Interpretation

of B. F. Westcott and Hermann von Soden.[15] Until the twenty-sixth edition, it was to these works the Nestle text referred.

Sources of the New Testament

Manuscripts

The first task of textual criticism is the approximate determination of the age of a manuscript. The first indication of age is the external form, that is, the difference between majuscule (capital letter) and minuscule (cursive, lower case). In contrast to ancient private letters, books were written in capital letters. Only from the eighth and tenth centuries onward did the cursive script prevail in Bible manuscripts. On the basis of form, of abbreviations, and on the basis of the writing materials used, the age of a manuscript can be determined with relative accuracy.

The book form yields a further indication of the age of a manuscript. In antiquity there were two book-forms: the roll and the codex. Since the New Testament manuscripts are all of the codex variety, the book-form as indicative of age does not apply. The normal writing material in antiquity was papyrus. Only later, when the community became more affluent, could use be made of the more expensive parchment, to say nothing of paper. In present day text-criticism, the papyri are indicated by the letter P and Arabic numerals, which refer merely to the series of registration. The mass of manuscripts are parchment codices. The older majuscule manuscripts are designated by capital letters: first according to the Latin, then the Greek, and finally the Hebrew alphabet. The four most important majuscule codices originally contained the entire Old and New Testaments. They include: Aleph = 01, Sinaiticus; A = 02, Alexandrinus; B = 03, Vaticanus, and C = 04, Codex Ephraim Syri Rescriptus (a palimpsest). All other majuscules contain only portions of the New Testament, for which the same letters are often used. There is a codex D which contains the Gospels, and another the Pauline letters. The minuscule manuscripts

---

15. Soden, *Novum Testamentum Graece*.

are numbered consecutively. The majority stems from the tenth or eleventh centuries. Their significance is considerably less than that of the papyri and majuscules. The best known minuscule is No. 33, the "Queen of the Minuscules." Finally, two groups of related minuscules should be noted, the Lake and Ferrar groups, or families 1 and 13. Finally, the lectionaries, the collection of pericopes designed for reading at worship, also have a certain significance.

Investigations of text critics have shown that many manuscripts indicate a clear relationship to each other, so that we may distinguish several "text families." The most important group includes the Egyptian, or the Alexandrian family. It is represented by majuscules Aleph, B, and C, as well as by A outside the Gospels. It was earlier assumed that a certain Hesychius edited this text a type, and thus critics spoke of the Hesychian text. The second group is the so-called "Western" text, so named because it is represented, among others, by the Latin translations. Beza Cantabrigiensis and Claromontanus contain such peculiarities as embellishments, in the Synoptic Gospels the tendency to approximate the texts of the individual Gospels to each other. Majuscule Theta, together with families 1 and 13, comprise the so-called "Caesarean text" family. The mass of manuscripts comprise the "Byzantine" text type, also called the "Imperial" or *Koine* text.

Versions or Translations

In addition to the Greek manuscripts, the old translations are of significance. The most important are the Syrian, Coptic, and the Latin.

Quotations from the Church Fathers

References to Scripture in the works of the church fathers yield material for textual criticism. (The division of the biblical books into chapters occurred in the thirteenth century and into verses by the Parisian printer Estienne in 1511).

PART III

Deciding the Condition of the Text ("Lower Criticism")

The Greek New Testament

As noted above, the Greek New Testament available to students and scholars is based on manuscripts in the original language, versions or translations, and quotations from the ancient fathers of the Christian church. For this reason, the Greek text is furnished with an apparatus in which each verse is attended by witnesses for or against a given reading, or, for an alternative. In the majority of instances, the apparatus will list the three types of witness, the members of which may belong to a "family." At present, the Greek New Testament used by the majority of scholars around the world is that based on the work of Eberhard and Erwin Nestle, edited by Barbara and Kurt Aland and their committee, and in its twenty-eighth revised edition edited by the Institute for New Testament Textual Research, and published by the *Deutsche Bibelgesellschaft* in Stuttgart, Germany.

A Brief Guide to New Testament Interpretation

Presuppositions of Textual Criticism

As indicated above, the transmission of the New Testament text is a history of corruption and intentional alteration. Until the invention of moveable type by Johannes Gutenberg (c. 1400–1468) it was virtually impossible to produce a text that barely approximated the originals. On this assumption or presupposition, and principally in the nineteenth century, there began the search for witnesses able to be mustered on behalf of a text that, arguably, harked back to the original drafts. Thus emerged the witness of the "three pillars": the papyri and codices, the versions or translations, and quotations from the Church Fathers. This presupposition still underlies the production of the various editions of the Greek New Testament, as the apparatus included with each verse indicates. The discovery over the centuries of members belonging to the "three pillars" has enhanced the assumption to the point that it is believed we now possess over ninety percent of the text coming from the hands of its original authors.

The Beginnings of Text Reconstruction

The story of the production of the Greek New Testament text harks back to the sixteenth century, a tale of the labor and commitment of hordes of scholars and researchers, now to the point where a majority is confident that we possess the New Testament in its original language essentially as it has come from the hands of its authors. The fact that the Nestle text has appeared in its twenty-eighth edition, testifies to the continuing labor of textual scholars and others struggling to decrease the distance between the New Testament author and the contemporary reader-interpreter. The task has been arduous, amid contest, conflict, and change. For example, the three "pillars" on which the English translation of the New Testament, authorized by King James I, rests, no longer belong to the earliest witnesses, centuries later come to light.

Deciding the Condition of the Text ("Lower Criticism")

Illustrations

John 7:37–39

To illustrate, the critical apparatus of the Nestle twenth-eighth edition offers four possible readings of John 7:37–39 and two of Rom 5:1. John 7:37–39 describes Jesus as standing at the last day of the festival and announcing that whoever thirsts should come to him, and whoever believes in him should drink; that out of the heart of such a one would flow rivers of living water. Then the evangelist adds, according to the NRSV: "Now he said this about the Spirit, which believers in him were to receive, for as yet there was no Spirit, because Jesus was not yet glorified" (John 7:39). In the other readings, one group of witnesses adds "the Holy Spirit."[1] A second reads, "the Holy Spirit on them."[2] And yet another reads, "the Holy Spirit was not yet given."[3] Scribes or copyists of the New Testament had to have been perplexed at the statement that "for as yet there was no Spirit." Lest the idea arise that the Spirit did not yet exist, modifications were introduced to remedy the problem. Introduction of the adjective "Holy" is a natural addition. More important, the temptation to add a predicate verb ("not yet given") could not be resisted. Clearly, the widespread and diversified constellation of witnesses for the reading as appears translated in the NSV ("for as yet the Spirit was not given") yields the reason for the other readings.

---

1. Papyrus 66, the Latin family of versions, uncial manuscript N with corrections, uncials W, G, D, 0105, minuscule manuscript. Families 1 and 13, 33, 565, 479, 700, 892, 1241, 1424, and the majority of *Koine* or Byzantine manuscripts.

2. Uncial D original with minor changes, minuscule 1 and Latin manuscripts.

3. Uncial Vaticanus, Latin manuscript, e and q, Syrian versions with slight variation from the Greek text.

A Brief Guide to New Testament Interpretation

Romans 5:1

The New Revised Standard Version of Rom 5:1 reads, "Therefore since we are justified by faith, we have peace with God." The Revised English Version reads, "Therefore, now that we have been justified through faith, we are at peace with God." But as the critical apparatus below makes clear, some authorities read, "let us have peace with God." These authorities, that is, the three "pipers" named above, include uncial (capital letter) manuscripts, minuscule (lower case) manuscripts, versions, or translations, and lastly the witness of an ancient church father (or in this case, a heretic, the Gnostic Marcion, (ca. 85–160).

The fact that the present printed Greek edition reads, "we have peace with God," does not decide the issue. The printed text functions to enable the student to begin at a given point. It is expedient; only useful until the final decision. As a matter of fact, the entire Nestle Greek Testament awaits the decision for or against, or alternative to what is printed.

As to Rom 5:1, the authorities for the reading "let us have peace with God" are equal in strength to the reading "we have peace with God."[4] When observed according to the external evidence,[5] the authorities for either reading have pride of place. Examination of the internal evidence[6] yields the same result. On the other hand, observance of the internal probabilities[7] decides

---

4. For the reading, "let us have peace with God," the uncials Sinaiticus (original reading), A, Vaticanus in the original, C, D, K, L, minuscules 33, 81, 630, 175, 1739 in the original, Latin witnesses divided, Bohairic, and Marcion (c. 85–160). For the reading, "we have peace with God," Sinaiticus second edition, Vaticanus, third edition, F, G, P, PSI, the probable reading of 0220, minuscules 1104, 365, 121, 1505, 1506, 1739 corrected, 1881, 2464, 1846 divided reading, mss. of the Vulgate differing from its most important editions.

5. When examined respecting their age, geographical distribution (how remote from each other) and genealogical relationship (belonging to a "family").

6. Preference given the more difficult reading; likewise to the briefer reading; in parallel passages, to the reading disagreeing with the others; attention given to what a scribe or copyist of the New Testament prior to the invention of moveable type, deliberately or inadvertently was liable to do.

7. Style and vocabulary of the author; immediate context; harmony with

Deciding the Condition of the Text ("Lower Criticism")

the issue. First, as to style and vocabulary, Rom 5:1 and the verses following comprise a song of praise in which the "we" style dominates. Romans 5:2 reads, "We *have obtained access* to the grace in which we stand." Romans 5:5 reads, "God's love *has been poured into our hearts* through the Holy Spirit *that has been given* to us. We also boast in our sufferings." The same style and vocabulary persist to the end of the song. It reflects a condition or situation already arrived at, as Rom 5:9–11 indicate: "Now that *we have been justified* by his blood" (v. 9); "while we were enemies, *we were reconciled* to God . . . surely, *having been reconciled*" (v. 10); "*we have now received reconciliation*" (v. 11). It is not until later that Paul writes what the believers should be and have, for the reason that the community must first be made aware of what it had received. Thus, the textual problem has been solved in theological fashion.

When all is said and done, the interpreter's conclusion regarding the truth or falsity of a reading depends on the answer given to a theological question. Here the question is: What has Christ done? Has he reconciled us and thus given us peace? Do his reconciliation and our peace belong together? Origen of Alexandria (c. 184–253), Chrysostom (c. 347–407), and Theodoret (c. 393–458/466): "Let us keep peace with God" *Pacem habemus ad Deum per Dominem nostrum Jesum Christum*. But is our peace uncertain? Has Christ's reconciliation been won, but our peace uncertain? According to the Apostle Paul, Christ has not brought about his readers' justification and left with them the concluding of peace, but with his justifying them has procured their peace. This will not be the only instance in which the textual problem needs a theological solution. The Greek New Testament contains many such instances.

---

the author's teaching elsewhere; the Aramaic background of a saying of Jesus; the priority of Mark's Gospel, and the influence of the Christian community on the formulation and transmission of the passage.

A Brief Guide to New Testament Interpretation

The Caveat

At least two things need to be kept in mind when dealing with the Greek New Testament, especially with the Nestle editions. The first is that the text is a *Studenten Ausgabe* (student edition), the decision for each reading dependent on the student or scholar's view of the evidence. This renders the text for all purposes an editorial "suggestion"; the final reading left to the student or scholar and thus open to debate. The assumption that the printed text is final can lead to confusion. Second, operating with witnesses according to a single "family" or group, as is indicated in the texts of Tischendorf or Westcott-Hort, as well as the earlier editions of the Nestle text, has been challenged in favor of a "horizontal" reading of witnesses across family lines, thus producing a text supported by the majority of all witnesses but always including the earliest witness, the Byzantine or *Koine* text type. This approach has been taken in the latest Nestle texts edited by Barbara and Kurt Aland.[8]

---

8. Cf. 'The Majority Text,'" in *Novum Testamentum Graece*, 14–15.

PART IV

Source Analysis

Definition

SOURCE-ANALYSIS IS PRIMARILY CONCERNED with whether and how the first three Gospels relate to each other in a literary way. There are striking similarities and dissimilarities between them. Agreement between the Synoptists reaches even to details of style and language. These agreements argue for dependence. But there are also divergences.

Presuppositions of Source Analysis

The striking similarities in the first three Gospels has led to the assumption of a literary dependence between them. Over the years this assumption has led scholars to assume that one of the three must have served the others as basis. The assumption that there is a dependence among them has not wavered since the nineteenth century. The same holds true of a second source, which can explain the similarities between two Gospels lacking in the other. The question respecting which of the Gospels furnished the basis for the other two is all but universally assumed, despite minority opinion, as well as the existence of a second source that explains the agreements between the two and lacking in the other, whether oral or written. The history of the so-called synoptic problem has birthed a riot of hypotheses regarding the similarities and dissimilarities.

The Hypotheses

The problem of their relation to each other becomes clearer when note is taken of older hypotheses. According to the traditions-hypothesis, advocated by J. G. Herder (1744–1803) and J. C. Gieseler (1792–1854), all three evangelists drew on oral tradition independently of each other. This hypothesis could not sufficiently explain the literary relationship between the Gospels. The use-hypothesis, advocated by J. J. Griesbach (1745–1812), assumed that one evangelist used one or more Gospels. This hypothesis could not sufficiently explain the differences between the Gospels. According to the ur-evangelium hypothesis, proposed by D. F. Michaelis (1717–91), and G. E. Lessing (1729–81), all three Gospels used an "Arch-Gospel" no longer extant. This hypothesis could not explain how the agreements between Matthew and Luke over against Mark could have occurred. It attempted to wriggle free of the difficulty by assuming that Mark had only an abridged text of the Arch-Gospel. The gragment-hypothesis of F. D. E. Schleiermacher (1768–1834) assumed the Gospels are composed of a great number of originally tiny fragments of individual stories, a hypothesis that failed to explain the total structure of the Gospels.

The Priority of Mark

The three synoptic Gospels have varying lengths. In the Nestle text, Mark contains about 1,500 lines, Matthew more than 3,000, and Luke more than 2,600. The situation is explained if it is assumed that Mark is the basis for Matthew's and Luke's Gospels; that Matthew and Luke undertook "improvements" on the Markan

Source Analysis

material and added further material, written or oral. Clearly, the decision regarding priority can only be made between Matthew and Mark, whereas Luke expressly acknowledges the existence of other Gospels prior to his own (cf. Luke 1:1–4). But it should be kept in mind that Markan priority has to do exclusively with literary relationships. The question whether Mark or Luke is older cannot be answered by source analysis. At any rate, the assumption that Mark's Gospel is prior, and that Matthew and Luke both used him, has been supported by a comparison of the total structure of the Gospels.

Illustrations

In Matthew's Gospel, John the Baptist appears in the wilderness, preaches from Isaiah, and his habit and diet are described. In Mark, the Baptist preaches from Isaiah, appears in the wilderness, the reaction of the crowds is described, as are also his habit and diet. In Luke, the Baptist appears in the wilderness, he preaches from Isaiah, there is no description of the reaction to this preaching, and his habit and diet are not described.

Agreements between Matthew and Luke against Mark

Obviously, Matthew and Luke contain a great deal more material than Mark, but the agreement between them exists only where they agree with Mark. Hence it may be concluded that Matthew and Luke worked independently of each other. Thus, Mark's Gospel served Matthew and Luke as a source. Mark is the oldest of the three Gospels. Note the following parallels:

Matt 5:3, 6, 11ff. parallels Luke 6:20–23
Matt 5:44, 39–42 parallels Luke 6:27–30
Matt 5:46f., 45, 48 parallels Luke 6:32–36
Matt 7:1ff. parallels Luke 6:37f.
Matt 7:3–5, 16–21, 24–27 parallels Luke 6:41–49

The Hypothesis

Although Luke and Matthew have no literary connection with each other, they appear to have used a source independently of each other, not known to Mark. These agreements cannot be explained as pure accident since there are agreements in structure. The simplest explanation is that there is a source Matthew and Luke used independently of each other.

Conclusion

This source, however, can only be hypothesized. The main content of this source consists of *logia* or words of Jesus, though also some narrative material. This source, dubbed "Q" for the German term Quelle (= source), may have been a floating layer of tradition, not written, and used by Matthew and Luke in a far different way than they used Mark. Assumed to contain *logia* and some narrative material, Q contains no passion narrative. However, the heaping up of individual *logia* in Q does not mean it occurred willy-nilly. Further, Q does not use the Messiah-title for Jesus, but it preserved Jesus' teaching and awaits his return. The place and time of Q's composition are unknown. Galilee and the area by the sea may have been the place of its composition and may have originated prior to Mark's Gospel.

The Caveat

The weak points in this "two-source theory" are as follows: a) How can one explain the fact that Mark contains a few sections not taken over by Matthew and Luke? b) If Matthew and Luke are not dependent on each other, how can one explain that in some passages they agree against Mark, though the substance of those sections originates with Mark? In such instances, reference is made to "minor agreements," which consist of stylistic or grammatical improvements. There are "doublets" in Matthew and Luke. That is, the same word of Jesus is transmitted in two different places. For

Source Analysis

example, Luke 8:17 appears also in Luke 12:2. In Matthew also this word is transmitted twice: in Matt 13:12 and 25:29. In addition to these single word doublets, there are discourse doublets. For example, Luke has two accounts of the sending of the disciples, one in chapter 9 and the other in chapter 10. This situation may be explained by assuming two reports of the sending, one in Mark, the other in Q. Problems remain. The original wording of Q can only be reconstructed with difficulty. Even the origin of the logia-source can only be defined approximately.

PART V

Form Critical Analysis

Presuppositions of Form Criticism[1]

THE CONTENT OF THE New Testament does not reflect a homogenous whole, but rather a wide variety of forms, some of which are easily identified; for example, the healing narratives, nature miracles, apocalyptic sayings, and the like. Attention to these forms protects against flattening out the contents of the New Testament, ending in an interpretation that treats every state or activity alike, disengaging its uniqueness or peculiarity. Further, each recorded event or saying, prior to the work of the evangelist, had a life, and in many instances was transmitted orally. Further, it is assumed that the life a particular saying or reading enjoyed lay in a community that nursed and transmitted it. The majority of scholars are content with identifying and attending to the variety of forms and in this manner preserving the distinctiveness they deserve. To this Rudolf Bultmann of Marburg was an exception, believing that he could trace a particular saying or doing to its original home (Palestinian or Hellenistic) and thus decide whether

---

1. This page and what follows includes an extended analysis according to the most celebrated form critic, Rudolf Bultmann, in Bultmann, *Die Geschichte der Synoptischen Tradition*.

or not it was genuinely historical or a creation of the community (*Gemeindebildung*).

The Task

The task of form-criticism is the analysis and interpretation of individual narratives, and at the oldest stage of the tradition. The search is thus for the smallest intelligible unit, since in the transmission of tradition addition rather than subtraction is more probable. It is an open question whether this smallest unit was transmitted in oral or written form. We recall that the Gospels are composed of independent, small units of tradition. Brief scenes (speeches, miracles, discourses) and parables are bound together by terse, "traditional" links. It is probable that these brief pieces were transmitted orally. Form-analysis thus investigates these small preliterary units respecting their external form, their content, and their purpose.

The Methods

Form-criticism employs two methods: an aesthetic and a sociological analysis. That is, it attempts to determine the external form of a text as well as the area or situation from which it arose. This explains why there is no universally recognized or unified nomenclature in form-criticism, and thus no unified analysis of the material. One scholar may proceed from the aesthetic point of view, defining the forms respecting their shape. Another works from the sociological point of view, defining forms according to their content. The question as to which method is correct is superfluous, since not nomenclature is at issue, but procedure.

The Laws of Style

1. In the story of gleaning on the Sabbath, how Jesus and his disciples came to the field, how long they were there, whether

or not they had a specific goal, and what was planted in the field, play no role at all. Only the fact of their journey is given, for the purpose of furnishing a framework for the speech.

2. There are scarcely any details. For example, in the miracle narrative the name of the person healed is not given (Bartimaeus in Mark 10:46 is an exception). Further details relating to time and place are often lacking. Description of the milieu is terse or totally lacking. Nothing is said of the motives of those involved in the action. When faith or joy is referred to, it is the faith or joy of the onlookers, not of the person healed (cf. Mark 2:5). The story intends to summon the hearer to faith.

3. In the conversations there are at times only two partners. For example, in Mark 2:1–12, Jesus, the people, the sick person, and companions are present, but Jesus' word is restricted to the sick person and to the brief debate between Jesus and his opponents.

4. Repression of all details in the New Testament narratives allows pointing first of all, and in every instance, to Jesus himself.

Speech Material

Apophthegms

To this group Bultmann assigns the apophthegms, subdivided into conflict and school speeches, biographical apophthegms, and the dominical sayings, in which Jesus appears as a teacher of wisdom, or proclaimer of prophetic and apocalyptic words, and creator of laws for the community. (The term "apophthegma" is used in the history of Greek literature and patristics, furnishing anecdotes about famous figures, climaxing in a pointed utterance.) The most important groups of apophthegms in the New Testament are the conflict and school speeches. The occasion may be a miracle, as in Mark 3:1–6, or a question directed to Jesus, as in Mark 2:23–28, to which, in good Rabbinic fashion, Jesus may reply with a counter question. The biographical apophthegms serve to render Jesus contemporary. Bultmann distinguishes organic and inorganic apophthegms. In the former, the word and scene are shaped in one breath; in the latter the word exists independently.

Dominical Sayings

Bultmann divides them into four groups:

1) *Logia* or words of wisdom (cf. Matt 12:34; 6:27; and 10:16)
2) Prophetic and apocalyptic words (Luke 6:20ff.)
3) Words of Law (Matt 10:11ff.)
4) "I" words (Matt 10:34–36)

The model for the *logia* is the Old Testament or Jewish aphorism. Form-critical analysis also yields certain points of view for the question as to which of the *logia* are to be regarded as genuine; that is, which can be traced back to the preaching of the historical Jesus. As soon as one removes their Christian, post-Easter framework, the question may be raised as to whether the *logion* stems from the teaching of the community, whether it fits the traditional framework of Judaism, or whether neither is the case, and it may be assumed that we have to do with an authentic word of Jesus.

Parables

The most important part of the speech material consists of the parables. The general characteristics are: terse description, only two persons involved, the action single and moves toward a goal, and the emphasis is on the conclusion.

A Brief Guide to New Testament Interpretation

Form-Analysis Outside the Gospels

Forms, such as confessions, songs, and fixed schemes are to be found not merely in the Gospels but also in the remainder of the New Testament, particularly in the Epistles.

The Forms of Synoptic Narrative and Speech Material

1. *Miracle stories.* This group is divided into healing and nature miracles. To it also belong historical narratives in which the miracle is the aim of the narrative. (Miracle narratives in which the point is not the miracle but a word of Jesus, belong to *the apophehgmata*: (Bultmann) or to the narratives (Dibelius)).

2. *Healing miracles.* To this group belong only those stories in which the miracle is the aim of the narrative. These stories have a typical structure: a terse description of the situation of the sick person, the demon recognition of the exorcist, the demon commanded to leave, the effect, and finally the effect on the audience.

3. *Nature miracles.* To historical narrative belong the baptism and transfiguration, and the birth, passion, and resurrection narratives, the latter distinguishable in two groups: the empty tomb narratives and the appearance narratives.

Form Criticism Outside the Gospels

1. *Confessional Formulae.* These comprise what may be the oldest stratum of the New Testament tradition.
2. *Criteria for reconstruction:*
    a. Occasionally, it is expressly stated in an Epistle that "tradition" or paradosis is cited (cf. 1 Cor 15:1ff.). This is

Form Critical Analysis

indicated by the typical catchword *paralambano* (I take) and *paradidomai* (I give).

b. The catchwords *pisteuein* (to believe) and *homologein* (to confess) may also refer to traditional material.

c. Certain external characteristics of style indicate the preference of traditional material.

- *Parallelismus membrorum* (parallelism of members) (cf. Rom 4:25).
- Relative style (cf. Rom 3:25).
- Participial style (cf. Rom 1:13f.).
- Peculiar vocabulary (cf. Rom 1:3f; 3:25), and such terms as *pneuma hagiosynes* (Holy Spirit), *hilasterion*, *paresis ton progegonoton hamartion*.
- A passage striking in its context may indicate traditional material.

3. *Results of attempts at reconstruction:*

   a. Confessions (the catchword *homologein*) relating to the person of Jesus.

   b. Statements of faith (cf. the catchword *pisteuein*), which relates to the work of salvation (cf. Rom 10:9, which contains both the homological and credal).

4. *Revelations-schemata.* A fixed scheme in which two distinct statements regarding the reaction of revelation to the world are set over against each other (e.g., God's plan of salvation was previously hidden; God's plan of salvation is now revealed), a scheme fully fleshed out in the Ephesian and Colossian letters.

5. *Songs.* Two songs after the style of the Psalms are clearly recognizable in the Magnificat (Luke 1:46–55) and the Benedictus (Luke 1:58–69). The following characteristics may betray the presence of a song: lofty style, strophic arrangement,

linguistic rhythm, and an accented position in the context (cf. 1 Tim 3:16; Phil 2:6–11; Col 1:15–20; and John 1:1–18).

6. *Other forms:*

   a. In early Christianity the Aramaic acclamation *Mara-natha* is used. Two interpretations are possible: the indicative (our Lord has come), or the imperative (our Lord, come). In the first case, the eschatological coming of Christ is at issue, in the second, his appearance in the assembled community.

   b. Primitive Christianity appropriates the "Amen" (cf. Rom 1:25).

   c. In preaching and teaching schemes are developed that can be taken as an expression of the Christian understanding of salvation.

   - The "once-now" scheme (cf. Rom 7:5f.), referring to God's gracious activity toward humankind.
   - The relation between the indicative and the imperative (cf. Rom 6).

7. *Forms of paraenesis.* That is, fixed forms derived from the environment of Christianity.

   - Aphoristic ethics after the Jewish model (cf. Proverbs and Jesus Sirach), each to be interpreted for its own sake.
   - Catalogues of virtues and vices modeled after Hellenistic Judaism, but hinting at Stoic origin (cf. Rom 1:29–30).
   - The *Haustafel* (House Rules) hint at Hellenistic origin but specifically Christian elements appear (cf. Rom 13:13–14).

Form Critical Analysis

Illustration

In Mark 8:27—9:1 appears Peter's confession of Jesus at Caesarea Philippi and Jesus' first passion prediction. Commenting on the passion prediction in 8:31, the majority argues that the prediction corresponds so completely in language, style, and sequence to Mark's narrative of the passion that the evangelist has trajected back into the mouth of Jesus the later account of his trial and death. In other words, the majority has taken this passage to be a "prophecy after the fact" (*vaticinium ex eventu*). In fact, it is difficult to compare the passion predictions with the narrative of the passion in chapters 14 and 15 without coming to such a conclusion. The similarities are hardly accidental. But it is not merely that such striking correspondence between the predictions and the passion narrative has led the majority to this conclusion. Use of the puzzling title, "Son of Man," has tended to reinforce the notion.

Assuming that these predictions are in some measure liturgical or credal would not rescue them from the eye of the critic but may carry us back a notch further than the majority has gone. The passion prediction is set within a "confessional context." The frame for this prediction in chapter 8 is Peter's confession. In all three synoptic Gospels the prophecy of the passion immediately follows Peter's acknowledgement of Jesus as the Christ. That this linking of the disciple's confession with the first prediction is not due to Mark's co-evangelists' allegiance to his outline, is indicated by the fact that the setting for Peter's confession is not identifiable in Luke. In fact, just prior to his narrative of the confession and first prediction occurs "Luke's Great Omission," his elimination of almost three chapters of Mark (Mark 6:45—8:26).

In each of his passion predictions Luke appears to follow the general pattern of Mark. Only before his prophecies of the passion does Luke omit or interpolate material. This renders Luke's independence over against Mark where he is assumed to be following him all the more striking, sufficient to arouse the suspicion that historical sequence and chronology are not always Luke's primary concern. The function of the passion predictions is not to yield any historical context, but to "interpret" the events, which are made to precede or follow them. Thus, the Christ confessed by Peter is interpreted as marked for suffering and death. Such an "interpretation," whether originally or subsequently affixed to the event interpreted, could have had its *Sitz im Leben*, or "situation-in-life," in a credal formulation of the primitive Christian community; to wit, a formulation reflecting that detection of such formulations enhances the historicity of a biblical narrative or that it detracts from its historicity would be an error. Transferring one's allegiance from the passion predictions as *vaticinia ex eventu* to the passion predictions as credal does not materially alter the problem. The prophecies are not more free of criticism in the one case than in the other. But the pursuit of this type of research makes clearer that point at which the contingent event in which the community believed it saw the hand of God and its understanding or conception of that activity came together. It is the *credo* that gives fact and faith their connection and thus makes impossible extracting nude facts from their interpretation or extracting their interpretation as an alien thing added to the fact. The *credo* is the reason why the fact is mentioned at all, and the reason why the interpretation has penetrated the fact. It is the *credo* that prevents viewing the contingent event in popular nineteenth century fashion, and also prevents taking flight into the sphere of the "idea." This, too, is a "fact." Israel, the Christian community's confession, is an essential component of the "factual" history.

The Caveat

First, scholars differ in their description of the form and content of the New Testament narratives and sayings. The choice of Bultmann's nomenclature intends merely to give an example. Second, the assumption that once the so-called "Christian framework" of the narrative or speech is removed, one may arrive at the point where it may be assigned to the Christian community or has to do with an authentic action or word of the historical Jesus, and further, to say the occasion or nature of the community that

Form Critical Analysis

transmitted it, is not shared universally. These factors have led to the abandonment of form- and redactions-critical analysis by the majority. Most scholars are content simply to identity forms of New Testament material without attempting to get back behind it to a supposed origin in the Christian community or with the historical Jesus, thus, to assess its genuineness.

PART VI

Redaction Analysis

General Comment

THE TASK OF THIS method is to elucidate the standpoint of the individual Synoptic Gospels. The question is under what viewpoint has the evangelist chosen and arranged his material? How has he worked the individual pieces of the tradition into the total context of his work? What theological tendency and intention underlie his Gospel? The earliest representatives of form-criticism regarded the evangelists as authors only to a slight degree, who functioned as collectors, transmitters, redactors. Redaction work may threaten form-critical work, though both do not compete but supplement each other. If the question of form-analysis reads: "What shape did the narrative or speech have prior to its being set in a context or structure?" then the question of redactions-analysis is, "What was the context or structure into which the narrative or speech was set?"

Redaction Analysis

Presuppositions of Redaction Criticism

Redaction analysis or criticism developed as a reaction to form-criticism, though logically it might have preceded it. The assumption of redaction analysis or criticism is that the New Testament is not a heterogeneous mixture that the various evangelists merely handed on. Such a view, argue the redaction historians, reduces the evangelists to the level of editors, mere transmitters, whereas each can be seen to pursue a particular goal with his work. For example, Matthew's five sections of his Gospel may be seen as reflecting the Deuteronomic collection in which Jesus follows in the footsteps of Moses; Mark draws a circle from the death of Jesus over the entirety of his life and career; Luke's two volumes, the Gospel and Acts, are constructed as an analogy for the unity of primitive Christianity, and John arranges the traditional materials available to him around the seven signs, from the miracle at Cana to the raising of Lazarus, followed, or preceded by, discourses.

Illustration

The author of the Gospel according to Mark has drawn the shadow of Christ's cross over the entirety of his life and career. In chapter one, the verb used for the arrest of the Baptist is reserved for the betrayal and arrest of Jesus. In chapter two, Jesus' answer to the question regarding fasting includes the *logion* according to which the bridegroom will be taken from them. Chapter three contains the first reference to Judas, Jesus' betrayer (Mark 9:19). In chapter four, following the parable of the sower, Jesus tells his disciples that they have been given the secret of the kingdom of God, but for "the outsider" everything is in parables for the purpose of rejection prophesied in Isa 9 ("In order that 'they may indeed look, but not perceive, and may indeed listen, but not understand; so that they may not turn again and be forgiven'" Mark 4:12). Chapter five is replete with references to tombs, drowning, sickness, and death. Chapter six reports the death of the Baptist. In chapter seven, spies come down from Jerusalem to entrap Jesus. Chapters eight, nine, and ten contain the three passion predictions. In chapter eleven, the authorities attempt to destroy Jesus. Chapter twelve contains the parable of the vineyard at the conclusion of which the death of the owner's son is plotted, a parable, Mark adds, that Jesus' hearers supposed he had taught about them.

In chapter thirteen, the "little apocalypse," there is reference to persecution, which is predicted for those who follow Jesus. Chapters fourteen and fifteen contain the narrative of the passion. In the final chapter of the Gospel the angel appears to the women announcing the rising of "Jesus of Nazareth, who was crucified" (Mark 16:6). Braided together with the death-motif is the so-called "Messianic secret." In chapter one, only Jesus sees the vision and hears the voice at his baptism. In the same chapter Jesus enjoins to silence the demons that know him: Mark 1:24–25, 34; cf. 3:11–12). In the same chapter appears Jesus' ambiguous use of the title "Son of Man" (Mark 2:10; cf. 13:24–26; 14:61–62). In chapter three he is described as insane by his own kith and kin (Mark 3:21; cf. 1:27; 2:7). In the parable of chapter four, the secret is compounded by its having been determined. In Mark 5:37 Jesus is confused with the Baptist.

In the move toward Jerusalem the secret does not break off. At Caesarea Philippi Jesus tells the disciples to tell no one about him (Mark 8:30). Passing through Galilee after the Transfiguration and cure of the boy with an evil spirit, he does not want anyone to know of it (Mark 9:30). In the passion predictions of chapters eight through ten, Jesus uses the title calculated to add to the "secret," the title "Son of Man," capable of three possible interpretations: a) as synonym for the personal pronoun; b) as a self-designation, or c) as another to whom he points away. It is possible to assume that this structuring of his Gospel in light of its conclusion, with the theme of the "secret" throbbing throughout, reflects the purpose pursued by Mark, thus a genuine author after a specific goal and not a mere transmitter.

Redaction Analysis

The Caveat

Although it is certain that the evangelist pursued a specific goal for his work, merely assigning to him the function of a transmitter is not at all accurate, nevertheless the attempt to determine precisely what goal the evangelist pursues with his work has led to a plethora of competing studies, yielding proof of the method's vulnerability.

PART VII

Lexicography

The Necessity

THE ILLUMINATION OF THE history and scope of the theologically significant words in the New Testament is an indispensable preliminary work for research into its theology. It is an error to devaluate linguistic research by way of concordances, lexicons, etc., for the sake of a definition from context, which leads to dogmatizing in interpretation.

Lexicography Presuppositions

Schools have run the gamut from viewing the Greek of the New Testament as the "language of the Holy Ghost" (J. Herman Cremer of Greifswald (1834–1903), *Biblisches-theologisches Wörterbuch der neutestamentlichen Graecität*) to the view that words as such have no meaning unless gleaned from a context (James Barr of Oxford, (1924–2006), *The Semantics of Biblical Language.)* Current scholarship differs from either viewpoint, which is liable to dogmatization. It further assumes that the language of the New Testament is a language on its way to decline from the Attic Greek

Lexicography

of the great literary and philosophical writers of ancient Greece, thus become common *(Koine)*, reflective of the marketplace. Further, it is assumed that the language of the New Testament reflects a dual environment, deriving from Palestinian-Jewish thought and Hellenistic religiosity. But given its "profane" character, the Greek of the New Testament enjoys uniqueness and peculiarity due to its service to New Testament thought.

History

Hermann Cremer, a systematician at the University of Greifswald, Germany, produced a *Biblical Wordbook of the New Testament* in 1867. His purpose was to treat the expressions of the spiritual, moral, and religious life in the New Testament in such fashion that the "organ of the Spirit of Christ" and the "language of the Holy Ghost" should be described. By comparing the language of the New Testament with secular Greek, and with the language of Hellenistic and Rabbinic Judaism, the differences and relationship of the biblical ideas would be shown. This spelled a complete rift between the language of the New Testament and the profane, Greek world, as well as the lack of any demonstration of development within the New Testament. In 1932, Gerhard Kittel (1888–1948) began the production of his *Theological Dictionary of the New Testament.*

Though building on Cremer's concern, Kittel attempted to allow the content of the individual concepts of the New Testament to become visible. Kittel emphasized that the historical character of the New Testament requires investigation of the Palestinian-Jewish as well as the Hellenistic milieu, adding that Hellenism gave coloration to Christianity. The assertion that the history of the theological concepts of the New Testament is essential to their application by the New Testament authors, and that research into this pre-history is essential to understanding New Testament theology, has been challenged. Not words, reads the challenge, but only sentences, can convey ideas. It is an error to dispense with lexicographical research. Since it obscures the traditions-historical scene and can lead to dogmatizing.

Illustration

In the "little apocalypse" of Mark 13, Jesus says, "When you see the desolating sacrilege set up where it ought not to be (let the reader understand), then those in Judea must flee to the mountains...." The phrase translated "desolating sacrilege" (*bdelugma eremoseos*) is from a rendering of the Aramaic *shiqqutz shmem* in Dan 9:27; 11:31; and 12:11; probably a reference to the heathen altar that Antiochus Epiphanes, "God Manifest" (Seleucid ruled from 175 BC until his death in 164 BC), built over the altar of burnt offering in 168 BC (cf. 1 Macc 1:54, 59; 6:7). The reference is thus to profanation. Some have held that the reference is to the statue that the Roman emperor Caligula attempted to place in the temple of Jerusalem in AD 41.

The Caveat

As stated above, keeping to the text in Mark 13, the fact that in Daniel the phrase appears in the neuter, whereas in Mark in the masculine, poses a problem. For this reason, most see in the phrase a reference to the anti-Christ, but the terms used and the parallel features in 1 Thess 2:3–10 suggest the manifestation of the anti-Christ in *a historical event*. The parenthetical phrase, "let the reader understand" is a dark hint. In a time of persecution, the reference to the temple needed to be cryptic ("set up where it ought not to be"). The reference to the sacrilege "standing in the holy place" in Matt 24:15 scarcely lifts the veil. The situation is like that of 2 Thess 2, with its reference to the "lawless one" and his restraining, or to Rev 13:18, with its reference to the "number of the beast," but more tense. Still, the fact that the reference to the anti-Christ implies a factual historical event (the attempt of Antiochus or Caligula) does not require restriction to only one single event. For Daniel

Lexicography

that "desolating sacrilege" could be identified with Antiochus, but for Mark with an entirely different figure. In fact, throughout the years, any number of enemies of the faith could have sat for the portrait of the anti-Christ. In the end, the interpreter is left with resorting to a definition that may or may not reflect the author's intent or purpose.

PART VIII

Sociological Criticism

Introduction

RESEARCH INTO PRIMITIVE CHRISTIAN social history, long ignored, has been renewed by scholars here, in Germany, and in Denmark. In these researchers a lack in New Testament exegesis has been made up for by a procedure that is more thorough-going from a scholarly point of view. Primitive Christianity began as a renewal movement within Judaism. The transition to Hellenistic Christianity or to Jewish Christianity was fluid. One datum serves as a rough criterion for dividing them. Hellenistic Christianity existed predominantly outside Palestine, while the Jesus-movement was a Palestinian phenomenon with influence on the neighboring Syrian area. The Palestine movement became an independent Jewish Christianity after AD 70. Until that time, it competed with other renewal movements within Judaism. After that time, Pharisaism gained the upper hand, while Christians were excommunicated. The Jesus-movement is thus a renewal movement within Judaism on Syrian-Palestinian soil, from ca. AD 30 to AD 70.

Sociological Criticism

Presuppositions

The primary presupposition of sociological analysis is that languages exist within systems. Accordingly, sociological analysis of the New Testament inquires into the system or systems reflected by its various witnesses. Further, this analysis assumes that the systems reflected in the New Testament are not *sui generis*, but derived from Greco-Roman society and its systems. The fishermen, tax collectors, centurions, and others who have left their mark on the New Testament witness reflect systems which match or collide. Accordingly, sociological analysis takes a dual approach: the one descriptive, identifying the various systems reflected, and the other explanatory, inquiring into the dynamics within each system. This analysis, its proponents contend, has been neglected, giving rise to interpretation of the language of the New Testament apart from a context determinative of it.

The Task

The task of the sociology of the Jesus-movement is to describe the typical behavior among persons within the movement, and its relationship to effects between that movement and Jewish-Palestinian society. This involves research into roles, factors, and functions:

1. An analysis of roles in researchers' typical behavior models.
2. An analysis of factors, their conditioning by the total society.
3. An analysis of functions and their effect upon the total society, of which there are at least four: a restrictive function or domestication; and a creative function or personalization.

Religion can be social cement or an impulse to renewal. It can inhibit or adjust; and can also assist toward independent action. All these functions can be detected in primitive Christianity. But it is clear that in no other religious phenomenon does the innovative function of religion appear so clearly.

A Brief Guide to New Testament Interpretation

The Methods

Whether or not a sociology of the Jesus-movement can be carried on depends on the sources and the relevant statements they contain. The source material is sparse, its exposition is debated, and interest in improving sociological details almost nonexistent. For this reason, all sociological data must be laboriously extracted.

Three types of extraction may be distinguished:

1. Constructive deduction evaluates pre-scientific sociological statements, which yield data concerning the origins, possessions, and status of various persons, or data concerning the program, organization, and behavior of entire groups.

2. Analytic deduction from texts, which indirectly yield sociological data. Such are statements concerning recurring individual events, conflicts between groups, ethical and judicial norms, literary forms, and poetic statements (cf. the parables).

3. Comparative deduction, which studies analogous movements in the world at that time. The broader type of behavior in their Jewish-Palestinian society, the more it may be supposed it was socially conditioned. For this reason, special attention is given other intra-Jewish renewal movements, such as the Essenes and zealots.

The Sources

The synoptic Gospels are the most important sources for the Jesus-movement, and the historical works of Josephus (c. 37–100) for the Jewish environment. In the Synoptics what is Hellenistic needs sifting out. Everything else may be used. The question respecting genuine or non-genuine Jesus-tradition remains open. If the genuineness of a tradition is assumed, it may be supposed that the transmitters shaped their life in accord with it. If it is assumed that it originated in the post-Easter period, then it may be assumed that the transmitters shaped the tradition in harmony with their life. In either case, the result is the same: there is correspondence between the bearers of the tradition and the tradition itself. A sociology of the Jesus-movement thus remains aloof from the conflict between "conservative" and "critical" interpreter respecting the authenticity or historicity of the tradition. It is untouched by the *aporia* of the Life-of-Jesus-Research, and yet contributes to its solution, for it suggests a continuity between Jesus and the Jesus-movement.

The Presuppositions of Sociological Criticism

The legitimacy of this research is contested. It is said that such research proceeds from a one-sided presupposition and hinders true understanding. One criticism is that sociology grasps only what is universal and ignores the particular. It is true that a sociological analysis is limited to universals. But it is also conscious, however, that the particular—the individual—may stand out all the more clearly the more the general or typical is grasped. A further criticism is that sociology reduces religious phenomena to non-religious factors. While it is true that sociology establishes more contacts between religious and non-religious phenomena than one's religion or Christian faith might wish, one-sided, causal derivation of religious phenomena from social data is only one possible interpretation of the evidence. The assumption of a mutual influence is much more to the point. In addition, it must distinguish genesis from value: From whatever soil an idea may originate, its claim to value is independent of it.

Regarding the propriety of a sociological analysis of the New Testament, this may be said: There is a universal attitude of curiosity stimulated by the very things covered by an aura of piety. Such an aura makes access to those things difficult, but this only obliges the interpreter to judge properly respecting the decisive events in one's history. Such judging and evaluating requires a knowledge of the historical and social contexts. Finally, there is the general question of human existence encountered in connection with the Jesus-movement. How is renewal possible, given all the social tensions of life, and without unleashing new, destructive forces? These interests and questions are legitimate, and the best way by which to do them justice is to be ready to correct one's prejudices, to be sympathetic to the fact that everything had two sides.

Illustration

Using the Gospel of Mathew as an example, it may very well be that its author is not the tax-collector Matthew-Levi of 9:9, but rather the scribe of 8:19 and 13:52. At any rate, Matthew appears to have been moderately educated, evidenced by his facility with the Greek language, his command of a considerable vocabulary with the frequent use of subordinate clauses and the genitive absolute. He may well have belonged to a Jewish-Christian circle of the more urban, sedentary type, witness his constant reference to "cities" and reference to Jesus' "house" in Capernaum. The Gospel of Matthew distances itself from references to Jesus' exorcisms and makes no mention of Pentecost. This suggests, if not an anticharismatic bent, at least a hesitancy toward the charismatic.

As to Matthew's community itself, most scholars reject portraying it as a group of wandering radicals, but rather an audience of Greek-speaking Jews, sufficiently affluent to be taken aback at the command to forsake home, family, and gods, thus tailoring Jesus' beatitude to read "blessed are the poor in spirit," rather than "blessed are the poor" as such (cf. Matt 5:3 vs. Luke 6:20). This suggests that Matthew's community was not identical with the earliest Christians but had attained a status frequently at odds with the synagogue, and taking its authorization from Jesus, for example, from his directive to pray in secret (cf. Matt 6:6).

Conclusion

Sociological analysis of biblical texts denotes a new direction in New Testament research and needs room for development. For this reason, it is important to emphasize that in this analysis the world

Sociological Criticism

of the biblical text must be carefully preserved, lest one fall prey to the illusion that the categories of interpretation, in this case of sociological analysis, are neutral. There is a vast difference between describing the communities of primitive Christianity sociologically, as simply sects, and describing them as religious minorities with a mission, and it is of great significance for Bible interpretation whether one employs analogy in unreflective fashion, or with some care and caution. Finally, in the new research we should not be pushed to false alternatives. It is not true that theological interpretation of the past confused the primitive Christian community with a theological seminary, or that it sublimated the faith of that community to kerygmatic doctrine. Teleological interpretation concentrated upon the history of primitive Christian preaching, and sociological research intends to bring to light the social conditions that accompanied and carried that history of proclamation.

The Caveat

Scholars who have used the sociological analysis have themselves issued a warning. One writes, "There is no single methodology proper to New Testament sociology. In this it is quite different from older approaches, particularly form criticism, which sprang virtually full grown at birth from one book . . . it is this systematic view of the *corpus deum* consistent with theological and methodological perspective which is still lacking in New Testament sociology."[1]

Another scholar writes of sociological categories after certain modern presuppositions that render them inappropriate for understanding antiquity.[2]

---

1. Best, "Sociological Analysis," 187.
2. Saldarini, *Pharisees, Scribes and Sadducees*, 1.

PART IX

Rhetorical Criticism

Definition

RHETORIC HAS TO DO with the artistic alteration of the normal flow of speech. Its purpose is to capture attention and thus motivate the hearer. Of interest to New Testament rhetorical criticism is its contribution to the interpretation of the formal structure of New Testament texts. The categories of ancient rhetoric that aid New Testament interpretation include:

- the *exordium* (beginning) *(captatio;* winning), the function of which is to arouse attention;
- the *oratio* *(propisitio)* (address/proposition), a description or sketching of the matter at hand;
- the *argumentatio* (appeal), the appeal to authority in quotations, sentences, arguments, examples, or comparisons; and finally,
- the *peroratio* (conclusion), summarizing the argument.

The peculiarity of the Pauline rhetoric, for example, is, at least in part, the uniting of Old Testament rhetorical figures with

Rhetorical Criticism

Hellenistic figures. This alternation between the two makes attention to the history of the figures necessary to their understanding.

Presuppositions

As noted above, rhetorical criticism assumes a virtual collapse of historical-critical method, due to the inability of its proponents to come to shared conclusions. Positively, it assumes an alteration of normal speech for the purpose of engaging the hearer-reader. It assumes the contribution of these figures to the formal structure of the New Testament texts. It further assumes that the categories of the combined Palestinian and Hellenistic traditions contribute to the understanding of these texts. Here, so reads the argument, is the greatest gain for New Testament interpretation. Rhetorical criticism thus takes a dual approach: first, that of identifying the various figures; second, that of suiting what figures are calculated to evoke what type of response.

Methods

To understand the rhetorical figures two procedures have been developed. The first involves examination of syntactical or semantic criteria, that is, word figures (*anaphora;* repetition), a series in which the first word is repeated (cf. the Beatitudes in Matt 5:3–11); figures in clauses (a "cumulus"), a heaping up of parts of clauses (cf. 2 Cor 6:4–10):

> As servants of God we have commended ourselves in every way: through great endurance, in afflictions, hardships, calamities, beatings, imprisonments, riots, labors, sleepless nights, hunger; by purity, knowledge, patience, kindness, holiness of spirit, genuine love, truthful speech, and the power of God; with the weapons of righteousness for the right hand for the left; in honor and dishonor, in ill repute and good repute. We are treated as impostors and yet are true; as unknown, and yet are well known; as dying and see—we are alive; as punished, and

> yet not killed; as sorrowful yet always rejoicing; as poor, yet making many rich; as having nothing, and possessing everything."

Note also Heb 11:32, in which a subject is merely alluded to:

> And what more should I say? For time would fail me to tell of Gideon, Barak, Samson, Jephtha, of David and Samuel and the prophets.

The second procedure involves the arrangement of figures calculated to produce emotional response, including figures for arousing attention (the allusion or *praeteritio* of Heb 11:32, or antitheses); figures for arousing affective states, such as appeals, wishes, intensifications, and figures of humor.

Illustration

In 1 Cor 1:8–31, the dominant rhetorical figures are antithesis and climax (heightening). Note, for example, verses 27–28 and 30: "God chose what is foolish in the world to shame the wise; God chose what is weak in the world to shame the strong; God chose what is low and despised in the world, things that are not, to reduce to nothing things that are.... Christ Jesus, who became for us wisdom from God, and righteousness and sanctification and redemption." Romans 5:3–5 contains a chain-conclusion: "...we also boast in our sufferings, knowing that suffering produces endurance, and endurance produces character, and character produces hope, and hope does not disappoint us." In these verses the connection is achieved by the verb common to each link in the chain, and by the object of the preceding link's becoming the subject of the link following. In Paul's letters "dialogical" or conversational elements often appear. Note, for example, the *prokatalapwe* or anticipation of the argument of its opponent in Rom 9:19 ("You will say to me then, 'Why then does he still find fault? For who can resist his will?'"). Note also the questions the apostle himself puts and answers with a "by no means." "What then are we to say?

Should we continue in sin in order that grace may abound? By no means!" (Rom 6:1–2a).

For Paul, especially, antitheses are of greatest importance for an understanding of Christian existence. Note Rom 6:12–14: "Therefore, do not let sin exercise dominion in your mortal bodies, to make you obey their passions. No longer present your members to sin as instruments of wickedness but present yourselves to God as those who have been brought from death to life and present your members to God instruments of righteousness. For sin will have no dominion over you since you are not under law but under grace."

Because of their numerous rhetorical elements, the New Testament apostolic letters can be termed "apostolic speech," which enjoys a peculiar affinity with the philosophical, doctrinal letter. These letters take up problems with biographical features. Note, for example, the argument in 1 Pet 3:5–6: "In this way long ago that the holy women who hoped in God used to adorn themselves by accepting the authority of their husbands. Thus, Sarah obeyed Abraham and called him lord. You have become her daughters as long as you do what is good and never let fears alarm you."

The rhetorical function of "sentences" deserves special attention. Sentences—pithy, pointed sayings containing briefly expressed thoughts—function not only as authoritative witnesses. Frequently, ideas are rounded off through sentences, and admonitions are often supported with brief sentences. A great part of schooling in antiquity consisted of learning maxims and sentences by heart. For example, Rom 12:24 and the parables have a rhetorical-argumentative function. Included among the rhetorical devices is the *qal-wahomer,* or conclusion *a minore ad maius,* the argument from the lesser to the greater. Note, for example, Rom 5:15, 17: "But the free gift is not like the trespass. For if the many died through the one man's trespass, much more surely have the grace of God and the free gift in the grace of the one man, Jesus Christ, abounded for the many. . . . If, because of the one man's trespass, death exercised dominion through that one, much more surely will those who receive the abundance of grace and the free gift of righteousness exercise dominion in life through the one man, Jesus Christ."

Ancient rhetoric defined kinds of text according to their objects, and distinguished judgment speeches, including accusations, defense, or more general arguments that something is good or evil. Let 1 Cor 9:4–6 furnish the example: "Do we not have the right to our food and drink? Do we not have the right to be accompanied by a believing wife, as do the other apostles and the brothers of the Lord and Cephas? Or is it only Barnabas and I who have no right to refrain from working for a living?" Appeals recommending or not recommending an action, or a more general admonition or warning, belong to this group. So also does so-called "partisan speech," inducing the hearers to take a stand respecting something to be praised or condemned. Note, for example, Phil 3:6: "As to zeal, a persecutor of the church; as to righteousness under the law, blameless." Or Gal 1:13–14: "You have heard, no doubt, of my earlier life in Judaism. I was violently persecuting the church of God and was trying to destroy it. I advanced in Judaism beyond many among my people of the same age; for I was far more zealous for the traditions of my ancestors." (Note also 1 Cor 5:14: "And God raised the Lord and will also raise us by his power.") Rhetorical influence derives in large part from the fact that the affections are addressed. In Paul the following emotive qualities are addressed: pain, joy, amazement, fear, shame, love, hatred, despising, and hope.

Knowledge of ancient rhetoric enables the exegete to recognize forms as the bearers of theological content. It teaches the exegete to understand the structure of linguistic forms in ways practiced in the time the texts were composed. In such fashion the exegete learns that forms have a history, and that even the language and concepts of an author can be judged in connection with those forms.

The Caveat

It should be no surprise that rhetorical criticism should have become the avenue to structuralism or post-structuralism. Its preoccupation with form and tone have been influential. But, as with its congeners, rhetorical criticism is tempted to abandon the fact that words have referents, that there exists a kind of transcendence by which words as such exist as mere letters unless they exist in reference to objects to which they refer. Johann Georg Hamann (1730–88), the great opponent of the Enlightenment era, called his friend Immanuel Kant (1724–1804), "the man of death," for his separation of thought from utterance, insisting that the objects of thought take shape in utterance. Again, according to the logo-centrist George Steiner (1929–2020),[1] words have referents because there is a God, the restriction of words to contexts in which they take their meaning not from beyond themselves but solely from other words in the same sentence or paragraph denotes a putting asunder what heaven has joined together.

---

1. Steiner, *Real Presences*. "The conjecture is that 'God' *is*, not because our grammar is outworn; but that grammar lives and generates worlds because there is a wager on God" (4); "We must read *as if*" (229).

PART X

Structural Analysis

Introduction

OVER THE YEARS, MALAISE increased over the viability of historical method. Its use resulted in a welter of interpretations and their irreconcilability. The result has been a flurry of methods. In this period appeared the so-called "structural" method by which the "synchronic" was opposed to the "diachronic" aspects of a given text or passage. Most importantly, structuralism is occupied with the entire narrative in order to inquire how an author appears in his text and lets his readers into it. The method favors "orality" over "textuality," rejecting preoccupation with the author's own goal. Exclusive attention is given the text, its words denied any referents beyond themselves. In structuralism's parallel method, "reader response" criticism, the text's autonomy is rejected in favor of the reader's creating or constituting the text.

Presuppositions

1. The first is the assumption that appearances are not reality. Phenomena are to be explained by phenomena below the

Structural Analysis

surface. Karl Marx (1818–83), for example, was convinced that surface events and phenomena are to be explained by structures, data, and phenomena below the surface. Specifically, social thought was to be explained and accounted for in terms other than that of conscious thought. For Marx, the social structure of a society was determined by its production conditions. Social relations are ultimately determined by the infrastructure of the society. According to Sigmund Freud (1856–1939), actions that seem accidental, unintentional, are determined by unconscious motives or mechanisms.

2. The second presupposition is that phenomena below the surface express themselves as codes. All human activities are coded expressions of the deep structures of the human brain. By decoding, one can discover the reality behind the appearances.

3. The third presupposition is that the deep structure of a set of different activities will be the same for all these activities. According to Claude Levi-Strauss (1908–2009), if we go on to compare two different societies, there will be a basic similarity between them, so that if one could uncover the proper laws of their transformation, that is, the laws that explain their divergence or variation, one could transpose the one set of systems into the other set.

The Aim of Structural Analysis

According to Levi-Strauss, since everywhere human thought reasons according to the same logic, it should be possible to uncover the structure of human nature itself.

The Implications

In order to break codes, one must pay attention to wholes. Further, at one pole is the literary text as it meets the eye. At the other pole are the deep structures that have been coded in the text. In between them are a series of intermediate structures of ever-increasing abstraction.

The Method

First, assign the major functional elements in a story to one of six different roles: subject, object, recipient, ordainer, helper, opponent. Second, when these roles are placed in relation to actions, one arrives at the following plot: a subject, aided by a helper and hindered by an opponent wantsing to possess an object or give it to a recipient; the object, and perhaps also the entire action, proceeding from an ordainer. Third, usually the outcome is arranged into a binary set: the subject does or does not possess the object, the recipient takes or refuses to take the object, etc.

The Benefits

1. The text is rediscovered as an object in its own right. The biblical text has suffered too long from diachrony, thus from historical relativism.
2. Biblical criticism scarcely sees the forest for the trees, scarcely sees the text for the individual traditions. Structuralism accents the principle of context. One must proceed from the fact that for the final author-redactor the text in all its parts is a meaningful whole.
3. The principle that words have only relative autonomy expresses the truth that meanings are not attached to words once and for all, but in great part are dependent upon their definition by the context.
4. The principle that the form has more than summary character is helpful. A form is not merely the result of the addition of subordinate forms; it rather has its own shape and its own meaning.

Structural Analysis

5. Universal concepts are necessary to understanding.

Illustration By Way of the Parables

The units of one New Testament parable may be represented by symbols (i.e., a, b, c, d, e).[1]

The critic analyzes other parables and arranges the findings, say, in a chart as follows:

Parable 1	a b c
Parable 2	a c d e
Parable 3	a b d
Parable 4	b c d e
Parable 5	b d e

Reading across, line by line, the chart shows the relation of one parable to the set. The deeper meaning is discovered only by comparing the parable with the entire set. But a serial (horizontal) reading will not yield the deeper meaning. Only when a serial reading is combined with a formal (vertical) reading, will the true meaning become clear. Going a step further, the critic produces a similar set for the entire parable genre. This final set will be the "generative" matrix from which all the parables derive, and by means of laws. For example, English sentences are "generated" from their matrix, i.e., the English language, and by means of the laws of grammar.

The structure is preserved or enriched by the interplay of these laws of "transformation," which never yield results external to the system. It is thus necessary to investigate the laws that control the development of the various levels and discover what may be called the "grammar" of the story. The final step involves comparing Jesus' actual parables with the "generative" matrix, and

---

1. I suggest the following schema: a=subject; b=goal; c=obstacles; d=enabler; e=inhibitor; as a way of tracking the component parts in a structural analysis of the parables of Jesus.

deriving conclusions, with respect to the distinctiveness of Jesus' style and message.

The Caveat

1. The important corrections and stimuli furnished by structuralism lie in the direction of universal principles, rather than in the concrete doing of exegesis. If structural universals are linguistic and anthropological constants that are valid beyond time, and—on the basis of the identical structure of the human spirit—enable understanding and translation and make it possible to reproduce texts with similar structure, the text of the exegete then consists in determining what structural scheme is to be applied to the text. This often occurs in forced fashion, and without care for the linguistic structure of the text.

2. The error does not seem to lie in the fact that one observes a text as reflective of a model, but in the fact that the number of possible models is fixed beforehand; that one appropriates without question, say, the model of Russian fairy tales, rather than gleaning models by way of tradition from the New Testament texts themselves.

3. Universal concepts are still historical concepts. The idea that "speech" and the "language" from which "speech" is generated as its matrix, together with the laws by which it is generated, has its roots in an innate, universal reason that assumes a monistic view of reality.

PART XI

Post-Structuralism Analysis

History

POST-STRUCTURALISM REJECTS THE ASSUMPTION of structuralism that it alone is sufficient for interpretation. If redaction-criticism led to reader response, according to which the reader "creates" the text, reader response led to post-structuralism, which asserts that with the other methods the analyst is tangled up in, what he or she is analyzing, and thus opposing, is a method. Binary thinking, such as in structuralism, is deemed oppressive, hierarchical. Further, speech is taken to be the paradigm for every form of presence and truth. Notable here is post-structuralism's opposition to method. In fact, it is designed to loosen the addiction to method.

Presuppositions

Post-structuralisms' power of description exceeds that of historical criticism. Post-structuralism regards the linguistic sign as arbitrary. According to Ferdinand Saussure (1857–1913), arbitrariness is the organizing principle of all linguistics. According to Jacques Derrida, (1930–2004), meaning is the product of difference; in language there are no positive terms. Differences are what make concepts possible. According to Michel Foucault (1926–84), at bottom everything is interpretation. There are no facts, only interpretations. The elements of language have no meaning. According to Jacques Lacan (1901–81), discourse is a dim reflection of the unconscious; the meaning of the text lies between a mirror and the observer, between the text and the reader. From this it may be inferred that the Gospel is a mirror in which one sees oneself. The more coherence the interpreter can ascribe to the text, the more confirming the self-reflection received back from it.

Illustration

In chapter four of the Fourth Gospel (John 4:4–26) Jesus' thirst at his encounter with the Samaritan by Jacob's well is the precondition for what is needed to satisfy spiritual thirst. Jesus, however, separates the spring water of Jacob's well from the living water after which the woman thirsts. The two levels should not have been separated but combined. The Samaritan woman, however, contradicts the contradiction, by indicating not what Jesus says, but by what he is. At his death, water and blood flow from his side. There the two levels are finally comingled. The flow of water from Jesus' side is thus a symbol, or metaphor, for the Spirit. And that flow of water does not occur with Jesus' presence, but his absence, i.e., at his death. Finally, the river of water is a river of desire, by which Jesus is driven toward union with the Father in his death, and by the Father himself who sent him into the world. For the Fourth Evangelist the metaphor of living water is the cosmos toward which parallels in the Gospel are drawn.

Caveat

The text has no priority in post-structuralism. Entirely aside from assigning priority to the text from a theological viewpoint, the text is already there before the reader or interpreter approaches it. To that extent, at least, the text has priority. Where there is no text, there is no interpretation.

1. The emphasis on orality vs. textuality overlooks the "eternity" of the written text. Speech or oral discourse is over with at the moment it occurs, but the text abides. It is noted, written down, and can last a thousand years.

2. In post-structuralism, the reader-interpreter undertakes the entire function of interpretation. In fact, there is no meaning apart from the reader. From a theological perspective, of the assumption of faith or of the operation of the Holy Spirit, interpretation is eliminated. But with the self a perspective, a point of view, a faith, however minimal or unconscious, is carried into the interpretation, no matter how accurately or poorly that self may be reflected in the "mirror" of the text. The interpreter brings an entire world with him or her into the interpretation.

3. Perhaps most strikingly of all, the illustration taken from Jesus' encounter with the woman of Samaria at Jacob's well, and the references to Jesus' death, are reminiscent of the approach of Origen of Alexandria and his successors, for whom the literal dealt with the historical event *(littera geta docet)*, the allegorical with what is to be believed (*quid credas*), the moral with what was to be done (*qid agas*), and the anagogic with what was to be hoped for (*qid spes*), and with the allegorical getting the upper hand.

PART XII

Reader Response Criticism

READER RESPONSE CRITICISM, LARGELY an Anglo-American phenomenon, came to full flowering in the 1960s and '70s with clues to its emergence in A. I. Ricards' (1893–1979) study in 1929 of the works of Samuel Taylor Coleridge (1772–1834), discussed in relation to the reader's emotional response. In the '30s, the analysis of Loise Rosenblatt (1904–2005) is arguably the first of the present generation of critics to analyze the reader's response to a given text. So also is C. S. Lewis. As early as 1926, with his *Chronicles of Narnia*, Lewis was indicating the role of the reader's imagination in engaging the text writing, for example, that "a poem unread is not a poem at all."[1]

Presuppositions

There are almost as many approaches to reader response criticism as there are advocates of the principle. There are the "individualists," due to their use of psychology as a starting point, who focus on the individual identity when processing a text. There are the "experimenters" who conduct psychological experiments on a defined set of readers. The experiments often involve free association

---

1. Cf. Schakel, *Imagination and the Arts*, 21.

during the study, with the *experimenters* collecting and interpreting "*reader responses*" in an informal way. There are the "uniformists" who assume the literary work controls part of the "response" and the "reader" the other part. Others see this position as internally contradictory, claiming that the "reader" controls the entire transaction. There are the "affective stylists" who view a literary text as an event occurring in time, coming into being as it is read, rather than an object existing in space. But, however they differ, the proponents of reader response criticism agree that the reader plays an active role in the interpretation of texts. This approach assumes that the traditional separation of reader and text, according to the subject-object model, in essence rules out the creative role the reader plays in interpretation.

Method

In general, the method employed by the majority of reader response critics includes the following (not necessarily in the order of their importance):

1. Close examination of the text in order to glean some meaning from it. In this instance, the interpretation is guided by the text.
2. Transaction with the text by bringing in past life experiences as aid to interpretation.
3. Concretizing the text by filling the gap between the implied reader (i.e., intended by the author) and the actual reader; in other words, between the artistic pole of the author and the aesthetic pole of the reader.
4. Confronting the reading as an ethical act. Comparing experience and moral beliefs with the narrative.
5. Complete the reading by bringing one's ethical position into play.

Illustration

What follows is the condensation of an abstract on Matt 24:3-29 by W. S. Vorster (1915-83), of the Union of South Africa, at a meeting of the Society of New Testament Studies (SNTS) in Bethel, Germany. The essay assumes that reading is an interactive process between text and reader; that the reading does something to the reader. Nor is its focus merely on what, but on why it is said.

The question is whether Matt 24:4-50 gives the answer to the disciples' question respecting the destruction of Jerusalem and the coming of the Son of Man ("When will this be?" [v. 3]). Once the reader is aware that Jesus is reliable, he/she has no trouble with his prediction of the future.

Jesus' reply begins with a directive ("See that no one leads you astray," [v. 4]). The phrase directs the reader to take an action, to be on the alert. The same occurs in vv. 6, 14-18, 20, 23, and 26, which structure the speech. The main thrust of the speech is thus to appeal to the reader to maintain a state of alertness, the effect to show that the events referred to are part of the plan of God. These events are not to be taken as occurring in the time of the disciples or the author of the Gospel, but are addressed to the reader, as is shown in v. 15 ("Let the reader understand."). The disciples' question may lead the reader to wonder whether the speech deals with both the destruction of Jerusalem *and* the appearance of the Son of Man. The term for "appearance" is used five times in Matthew, and only in this chapter, indicating that the appearance of the Son of Man is the formative principle of the speech. From his/her reading of the Gospel the reader knows Jesus is the Son of Man.

Assuming a *caesura* between verses 2 and 3, the one dealing with the destruction of Jerusalem, the other with the coming of the Son of Man, the conclusion to be drawn is that Jesus flouts the question of the disciples, not wanting to pursue the topic of Jerusalem's destruction any further. The disciples are thus set in a different perspective than that familiar to the reader. By the end of the speech the attentive reader would realize that Jesus has defamiliarized the familiar by speaking of his return, not about the destruction of Jerusalem and its temple. It is a de-familiarization, which acquaints the reader with the novelty in the story of Jesus. The expectation of the disciples is thus disappointed, instead of which they receive the injunction to be on the alert.

This focus on what texts do, and not on what they mean, is an aspect neglected in New Testament interpretation.

Caveat

Reader response criticism is not for the tyro or novice who supposes he/she may interpret texts in any way at all, the reader *contra mundum*. The essay of Stanley Fish of Yale, Columbia, and Duke (1938–), *Is There a Text in This Class?*[2] responds to a question put to him by a student in his class, devoting considerable space to counteracting the so-called "New Criticism," which allows no authority to author or reader. To the student's question, which could just as well have been, "Do we believe in poems, or is it just us?" he initially disputes the separation of the reader from the text according to the object-subject model, then argues that the different perspective options have palpability and space only because of the assumption of me or other systems of intelligibility.[3] Fish continues that no one's interpretations are exclusively his/her own but "fall to him by virtue of his position in some social organized environment."[4] That is, one's interpretation will always be shared and public; meanings having their source in the interpretive community. Irresponsible interpreters will not be allowed to overwhelm their texts.

Earlier, Louise Rosenblatt had written that readers transact with the text by bringing in their life experiences to help interpret the text.[5] And C. S. Lewis had rhapsodized on the power of the imagination in engaging texts, but that such was not itself a moral

2. Fish, *Is there a Text in this Class?*
3. Fish, *Is there a Text in this Class?*, 331.
4. Fish, *Is there a Text in this Class?*, 335.
5. "Louise Rosenblatt." Cf. the section on "Research and Contributions."

activity, but it could be made to serve it.⁶ In her introduction to the essays in *Reader-Response: From Formalism to Post-structuralism,* Jane Tompkins of Temple, Duke, and Chicago (1940–) writes that the reader remains all-powerful in interpretation, but once he/she begins to read becomes the prisoner of the author's consciousness;⁷ that the reader's creativity is proof of the inexhaustibility of the text.⁸ She refers to "rules" that constrain production, range, and direction of the reader's response;⁹ that interpretation is a process determined by the community of interpreters;¹⁰ a process constituted by one's own interpretive categories that are public and shared.

---

6. Cf. Schakel, *Imagination and the Arts,* p.
7. Thompkins, *Reader-Response Criticism,* xvi.
8. Thompkins, *Reader-Response Criticism,* xvii.
9. Thompkins, *Reader-Response Criticism,* xvii.
10. Thompkins, *Reader-Response Criticism,* xxi.

PART XIII

Feminist Analysis

History

THE FEMINIST INTERPRETATION OF the Bible has not been without precedent. Sarah Grimke (1792–1873), born in South Carolina, educated at Yale College, pointed to the masculine bias of biblical interpretation as part of a deliberate plot against women. Catherine Beecher, daughter of the famous Lyman Beecher, Presbyterian minister (1800–1878), proposed women's suffrage in *The True Remedy for the Wrongs of Women* and *Woman Suffrage and Woman's Profession* (1871). In 1895 Elizabeth Cady Stanton (1815–1902) and eighteen other suffragettes published "The Woman's Bible," stating that the Bible was the "stone of misogynistic religion and of women's oppression."[1]

In these latter years, one factor has been the ordination of women in the 1970s, which, at least in the so-called liturgical denominations, required attention to biblical texts assigned to the Sundays of the liturgical year. Deconstruction also had its uses for feminist interpretation. Stephen D. Moore notes that deconstruction led some to enlist in their battle against "historical essences"

---

1. Russell, *Feminist Interpretation*, 14.

such as "woman."[2] Others, however, opposed the Derridean or deconstruction method as male dominated and gave attention to matters of gender, race, and color. But whether for or against it, deconstruction furnished an impulse toward feminist interpretation. Liberation theology also furnished stimulus. In 1979 a working group of the American Academy of Religion and the Society of Biblical Literature focused on "The Effects of Women's' Studies on Biblical Studies," and in 1984 the national Council of Churches' task force appended an "Inclusive Language Dictionary" to the Revised Standard Version of the Bible. Among the most celebrated feminist interpreters are Elisabeth Fiorenza (1938–), Barbara Johnson (1947–), Rosemary Reuther (1936–), Letty Russell (1929–2007), all of Harvard, and Phyllis Trible (1932–) of Union Theological Seminary.

Presuppositions

Feminist interpretation assumes the marginalization of women in the Bible for the sake of male patriarchy and damaging women's humanity. It assumes that God is active in the process of "new creation" (i.e., a more perfect creation here and now). Just as Jesus reinterpreted the Old Testament, so may the feminist. Accordingly, the Bible is to be read within its sociological and cultural context. This is the context in which the "male narrative" is but a part of the creation in a hierarchy with the male at the top. Thus, the need to challenge biblical interpretations that reinforce male domination. This means reconstructing the "hidden history" of "losers" (oppressed peoples and classes). For many feminist interpreters what is to be retained is the prophetic and liberating story of God's concern for the oppressed and the mending of creation among communities of faith. One interpreter, however, writes that the Bible must be left behind to focus upon the sacrality of women and seek to recover the rich religious insights of Goddess traditions. Further, feminist interpretation involves commitment to the

---

2. Moore, *Poststructuralism*, 26.

Feminist Analysis

poor and marginalized, to whom the good news is addressed as a way of extending the hoped-for horizon of God's new creation and its theological-ecclesiastical traditions. Finally, as one interpreter writes: "A feminist critical consciousness does not always state positively what it stands for, but it knows and names its enemies . . . by tearing down many of the old patriarchal buildings."[3]

Method

Feminist interpretation has developed in two areas: a) in the area of inclusive language; and b) in the area of inclusive interpretation. It challenges the impact of patriarchal tradition in the lives of women and confronts the divinely sanctioned patriarchal view of the world as the basis of religious security. According to Elisabeth Fiorenza, whatever denies, diminishes, or distorts the full humanity of women, is to be appraised as nonredemptive. Only the nonsexist and nonandrocentric traditions of the Bible and the nonoppressive traditions of biblical interpretation have the theological authority of revelation.[4] The patriarchal view is to be challenged by "a paradigm of emancipatory praxis."[5]

In a reflection on the ordination text of Gal 3:28, Antionette Brown of Oberlin (1825–1921) wrote that feminist consciousness called for "discrimination between those parts of the Bible that were essential and those that were relative."[6]

Illustration

Commenting on Isa 60:12 ("For the nation and kingdom that will not serve you shall perish; those nations shall be utterly laid waste"), the feminist interpretation sees an example of prophetic criticism and hope in Jesus' interpretation of the text in Luke 4:18

---

3. Cf. Russell, *Feminist Interpretation*, 27.
4. Cf. Russell, *Feminist Interpretation*, 13.
5. Cf. Russell, *Feminist Interpretation*, 16.
6. Cf. Russell, *Feminist Interpretation*, 23.

("with many other exhortations, he proclaimed the good news to the people"). The ancient text promised renewal of the ancient promises of messianic hope but also the nationalistic triumph of Israel over the Gentiles (cf., Isa 61:5–7: "Strangers shall stand and feed your flocks, kingdoms shall till your land and dress your vines; but you shall be called priests of the Lord, you shall be named ministers of our God; you shall enjoy the wealth of the nations, and in their riches you shall glory. Because their shame was double, and honor was proclaimed as their lot, therefore they shall possess a double portion; everlasting joy shall be theirs"). Here "Jesus' word" regarding Scripture as "fulfilled in our ears" (Luke 4:21) evokes admiration and praise from the hometown folks. He then launches into a reinterpretation of the text and the mood shifts dramatically. He interprets it as good news and healing that will come not to Israel but to the Gentiles and, indeed, to women and lepers among the Gentiles (Luke 4:25–27). Such constitutes a prophetic reversal of interpretation of the text, calculated to call the people in the synagogue from their chauvinism. "Jesus thus does not repeat the interpretation of the text in Isaiah but reverses it in order to make critical points that God is calling people to hear. . . . Today, Christians would repeat Jesus' interpretation as triumph of Gentile Christianity over the particularism of Judaism, an attack on Israel rather than a call to Israel to widen its perspective. . . . The feminist interpretation of prophecy as feminist critique thus continues the process of a critical hermeneutic whereby the text is interpreted in the context of the new communities of critical consciousness."[7]

Caveat

It is indeed true that in society, culture, professions, and religion, women have been marginalized. It is also true that they should be wrested from such contexts to enjoy equality with men. With such scholars as Fiorenza, Reuther, and others, enlisting Jesus in the criticism of patriarchy and its exclusivity in favor of universality is

---

7. Cf. Russell, *Feminist Interpretation*, 122.

Feminist Analysis

welcome, and no doubt overdue. In the interpretation of the Bible, however, several things need to be kept in mind when attacking male domination in the biblical record. Israel was surrounded by a welter of religions, which involved sexual orgies and human sacrifice in the name of female deities. To distinguish Israel's faith from, for example, Canaanite worship, in which the goddess Astarte vied for equal status with Baal, or from Greek and Roman religion with their plethora of gods and goddesses such as Demeter (Roman: Cees), Athena (Roman: Minerva), and Artemis (Roman: Diana), it had to happen that use, and in some instances exclusive use, of the male pronoun Jahve or El ("God"), Eloah ("God"), or "I AM," Tzervaot ("Lord of hosts") was sorely needed.

What distinguished Israel's God from the surrounding deities was not merely gender, but the fact that ultimately the name of God could not be uttered, let alone erased when written. This very practice was calculated to loft the name of God beyond the gender or sexuality of the Gentle deities; a factor often missed in feminist criticism of the patriarchal nature of biblical religion. And it is this characteristic that renders the attraction for the goddesses of other religions a descent into the gender and sexual exclusiveness that feminism is designed to critique. Secondly, it is necessary to keep in mind that with Assyrian, Babylonian, Persian, Greek, and Roman domination of Israel, there was an equality of suffering on the part of male and female Israelites. It was to this equality of suffering that Isa 61, for example, gave hope, and for this reason Jesus chose it, despite his reversal of its triumphalism.

Finally, with its critique of male domination in theology and ecclesiology, the feminist movement in the church ought not to forget that despite whatever aberrations may exist in the biblical record, what lies at its heart is that God came down in human flesh to save the world he loved, and that is what distinguishes it from every other persuasion, past or present, ancient or modern.

SUMMARY

The Preacher's Burden[1]

The Task

ASIDE FROM ITS ORIENTAL, enigmatic character, the history of the Bible's transmission, at least until the invention of moveable type, is a story of deliberate or unconscious corruption. For this reason, the exposition of a portion of it requires a modicum of acquaintance with the fact that portions underwent revision throughout the history of its transmission so as to facilitate a decision regarding its probable status. Further, inasmuch as the several books of the Bible—particularly the Synoptic Gospels, which have the lion's share in any pericope system—enjoy a relation to each other, it is necessary to be aware of similarities and dissimilarities between the books in question, and to arrive at some appropriate scheme respecting the origin of such phenomena.

The interpreter also needs to be aware of the pre-literary stage at which Christian traditions developed, of the conditions that determined the formation of those traditions culminating in the written Scriptures. Further, the interpreter needs to consider the possibility that the author amended, enlarged, and engaged in

---

1. Cf. Introduction to Stuhlmacher, *Historical Criticism*, 7–15.

reflection on what he inherited. The interpreter also needs to pay attention to the words of the text and their meanings. Since no exposition of texts can succeed without setting them within the larger historical perspective, the interpreter needs acquaintance with literature and movements contemporaneous with the Bible, and to set the literature of the Bible within an ordered whole.

Finally, there is the preacher's or interpreter's most agonizing task: that of climaxing his or her work by actualizing the text, rendering it contemporary for the hearer in the hearer's own language and thought forms.

Reactions

In face of this task as standing between the text and the hearer, two main reactions may be noted:

1. The first consists of an abandonment of the various approaches to the text in a haste to achieve relevance. In that case, it is not "the text for the day" that is actualized, nor the biblical world that is translated into the hearer's idiom. The gravest result of this practice is that the concept of Scripture as the vehicle of God's encountering, demanding claim, of the Word of God as not merely *ex post facto* illuminating, but as itself radically constituting the problem of human existence, is abandoned. In this case, the Bible is no longer the initiator of the human dilemma.

2. The second reaction consists of arduous application to the problems of textual, literary, and historical research, coupled with the refusal to shoulder the burden of actualizing the text. "With all the intense preoccupation with the text, such a preacher/interpreter seldom gets out of Palestine."[2] That is, earnestness in the matter of what is viewed as devotion to the text forbids the text's taking on the preacher's/interpreter's own flesh. One result of this reaction is that whereas

---

2. Rev. Roy A. Harrisville Sr., Minneapolis, Minnesota, anecdote heard by the author.

the biblical contents are generally known, the question of their relevance to the contemporary situation is left open. A gulf is fixed between the Christus *crucifixus* and the *Cristus Praesens*; faith is then treated as assent to an event of the past.

It is by encounter with the Christ present through the biblical word that the preacher/interpreter dares to equip with the flesh and blood of his or her own existence as well as that of the hearer, and that God's redemptive activity in our yesterdays acquires true significance. If the first type of reaction spawns a dead book, the second begets a dead interpreter.

Toward a Solution

It has often been stated that the solution to the problem lies in coupling the two types of reaction. Part of the solution lies in the preacher's/interpreter's recapturing appetite for the task, and recognition of the homespun truth that the Bible is people. It is not first of all events, occurrences, and happenings that comprise the canonical Christian collection, but a chorus of the voices of people: people without patience ("Oh, Lord, how long shall I cry for help, and you will not hear?"); people in anguish or despair ("My God, my God, why have you forsaken me?"); people who hope ("In everything God works for good with those who love him"); and people who dream ("Then I saw a new heaven and new earth"). What, or rather *who*, furnishes the occasion for these expressions gives peculiarity and uniqueness to this collection of voices. It is not their hoping or doubting, their anguish or dreaming, that separates them from the ordinary person. What has occurred to them does not render them more than human. There are, in fact, times when they exhibit what is primitive or inhumane ("Let them be put to shame and confusion altogether who seek to snatch away my life; let them be turned back and brought to dishonor who desire your hurt!"). The simple recognition that in proceeding to the "text for the day" one is not dealing with an object—but with a person—is the dawn of interpretation. When the preacher/

interpreter comes alive to the fact that interpretation is conversation between persons, interpretation can only be described as the result of genuine companionship.

Obviously, since texts with whom the interpreter converses are no longer alive, the nuances of feeling and expression normally conveyed in gesture, tone, and facial feature are lost. The distance of the years over which dialogue between author and interpreter occurs places the interpreter at a disadvantage. But it is precisely for this reason that the task of telescoping that distance that biblical criticism with all its components was born. These tools are not to be acquired and used for their own sake, as though determining the meaning of a word with the history of its usage spelled interpretation. Nor are they to be spurned by the "practical" person as belonging exclusively to the specialist. They are the proper aids to conversation, requiring to be used to the limit by pastors and teachers who cannot be content with hearing broken bits of their biblical companions' conversation, but whose calling and thus whose joy require that they hear as much as it is humanly possible to hear.

Discourse—allowing one's biblical conversation partner to speak—requires, in addition to the learning of the partner's "language," a quality sometimes called "divination" or "intuition." The mind and heart coming to expression in the text cannot be heard and understood purely by means of interpretive "rules," however time-honored. In genuine dialogue, each partner does assent to the quality of the spontaneous and even irrational residing in the habit and thought of the other. That admission is more in the nature of the acknowledgement of the other's humanity or personhood, and hence of the other's individuality; more a case of "live and let live" than anything else. But for such acknowledgement to occur, each requires the soul—if not the talent—of a poet. In that recognition, in that awe and wonder before the other, conversation reaches to its deeper levels. Indeed, such recognition is the ultimate goal of all genuine discourse.

The other side of the coin is that the preacher/interpreter needs also to have his or her chance to speak. He or she cannot stand mute before the text, for it requires one's own speaking to achieve its intention. If conversation with one's author requires the learning of the author's language and the acknowledgement of the author's identity, it also requires that one addresses the partner from out of one's own passions. This is the way of the gospel writers themselves. They have not left the tradition untouched or unadorned. With all their faithfulness to Christ, their perspectives have influenced the selection and arrangement of the material to a degree that renders search for an object amenable to pure research almost impossible. Matthew's "five books against the Jews," Mark's "book of the secret epiphanies," Luke's historiography, and John's signs and discourses reflect their own role in the encounter with Jesus Christ. If their faith had not been thus expressed, if the tradition had not taken on their own blood and bone, their Gospels would not have been kerygma, but biography. There is scarcely one single narrative or speech recorded in the Gospels, or in all the New Testament, which has not in some way—by virtue of arrangement within a larger whole, or of downright transformation—become the writer's own story, his own word.

Similarly, the preacher/interpreter needs to give his or her own flesh to the biblical word before it can take on life for the hearer. One's own inquiry after God and the meaning of human existence, one's own anxiety and despair, observation, and hope, needs to be added to that word before proclamation or interpretation can occur. Years ago, Karl Barth put it more eloquently: "Intelligent comment means that I am driven on till I stand with nothing before me but the enigma of the matter; till the document seems hardly to exist as document; till I have almost forgotten that I am not its author; till I know the author so well that I allow him to speak in my name and am even able to speak in his name myself."[3]

There is nothing to do but to respect the axiom—preaching is the audible, palpable expression given to a covenant of voice with voice, the congealing of the proclaimer's conversation with the biblical witness, a reflection of the excitement in converse with the text. And, in midst of this conversation and its reflection, the living

3. Barth, *Epistle to the Romans*, 18.

God appears. Not as one principally to be remembered, though indeed the discourse with the author involves taking up past deeds, but the word unflushed in the preacher/interpreter's coexistence with the ancient witness encounters the hearer as a contemporary. By means of that conversation of interpreter with the biblical witness occurs the encounter with Jesus Christ himself.[4]

---

4. Barth, *Epistle to the Romans*, 8.

Glossary

A minore ad maius. From the smaller to the greater.

Allegory. The representation of abstract ideas or principles by characters, figures, or events in narrative, dramatic, or pictorial form.

Anaphora. The repetition of a word or phrase at the beginning of successive clauses.

Apologetics. The religious discipline of defending religious doctrines through systematic argumentation and discourse (Wikipedia).

Apophthegma. A short, pithy saying.

Aporia. An insoluble contradiction or paradox in a text's meanings.

Arian Controversy. The Arian controversy was a series of Christian theological disputes that arose between Arius and Athanasius of Alexandria, two Christian theologians from Alexandria, Egypt. The most important of these controversies concerned the relationship between the substance of God the Father and the substance of His Son (Wikipedia).

Augsburg Confession. The Augsburg Confession, also known as the Augustan Confession or the Augustana from its Latin name, *Confessio Augustana,* is the primary confession of faith of the

Glossary

Lutheran Church and one of the most important documents of the Protestant Reformation (Wikipedia).

Catenae. A closely linked series of writings.

Codex. A manuscript volume of Scripture.

Commentary. Exposition of an entire biblical text.

Concordance. Alphabetical index of words used in a text or manuscript.

Corpus Christi. The body of Christ.

Credo. A creed.

Deist. A religious belief holding that God created the universe and established rationally comprehensible moral and natural laws but does not intervene in human affairs through miracles or supernatural revelation.

Dicta probantia. Proof texts.

Epistles. Letters written by the Apostles.

Exegesis. Critical explanation or analysis, especially of a text.

Fanatics. A person marked or motivated by an extreme (unreasoning) enthusiasm, as for a cause.

Fragment hypothesis. The idea that the Pentateuch and the book of Joshua have a common core, but have been added to at various times. (www.quora.com)

Gemeindebildung. Creation of the community.

Gematria. A numerical system used in kabbalah and other forms of Jewish mysticism that assigns numerical values to words based on the fixed numeral values of their letters.

Glossary

Gnosticism. The doctrines of various religious sects flourishing especially in the second and third centuries AD in the Near East, teaching that the material world is the imperfect creation of a subordinate power or powers rather than of the perfect and unknowable Divine Being, and that the soul can transcend material existence by means of esoteric knowledge.

Haustafel. House rules.

Heilsgeschichte. Salvation history.

Homily. A sermon, especially one intended to explain the practical and morel implications of a particular scriptural passage.

Humanism. A cultural and intellectual movement of the Renaissance that emphasized human potential to attain excellence and promoted direct study of the literature, art, and civilization of classical Greece and Rome.

Koine. "Imperial" Greek. A dialect of Greek that developed primarily from Attic and became the common language of the Hellenistic world, from which later stages of Greek are descended.

Logion (pl. *logia*). A saying attributed to Jesus in the Gospels or in other ancient sources.

Majuscule. Capital letter.

Messianic. Of or relating to Jesus as the Messiah.

Miniscule. Cursive, lower case.

Paraenesis. Fixed forms derived from the environment of Christianity.

Patristics. The study of the lives, writings, and doctrines of the Church Fathers.

Pericope. An extract or selection from a book, especially a reading from Scripture that forms part of a church service.

Glossary

Philology. Literary study or classical scholarship.

Pietism. A reform movement in the German Lutheran Church during the 1600s and 1700s, which strived to renew the devotional ideal in the Protestant religion.

Platonism. The philosophy of Plato, especially insofar as it asserts ideal forms as an absolute and eternal reality of which the phenomena of the world are an imperfect and transitory reflection.

Polemics. The art or practice of argumentation or controversy.

Postil. A commentary or marginal note in the Bible.

Praeteritio (Apophasis). Allusion to something by denying that it will be mentioned.

Prokatalapwe. Anticipation of the opposing argument.

Quelle. Source.

Qumran. An ancient village in Palestine on the northwest shore of the Dead Sea in the West Bank east of Jerusalem. It is noted for the caves in which the Dead Sea Scrolls were found.

Reformation. The Protestant Reformation was a major movement within Western Christianity in sixteenth-century Europe that posed a religious and political challenge to the Catholic Church and in particular to papal authority, arising from what were perceived to be errors, abuses, and discrepancies by the Catholic Church (Wikipedia).

Sache. Subject matter.

Scholasticism. The dominant form of theological and philosophical study in Western Christianity in the Middle Ages, based on the authority of the Latin Fathers and of Aristotle and his commentators.

Glossary

Scholia. Scholia are grammatical, critical, or explanatory comments—original or copied from prior commentaries—which are inserted in the margin of the manuscript of ancient authors, as glosses. One who writes scholia is a scholiast.

Sectarian. Adhering to or confined to the dogmatic limits of a sect or denomination; partisan.

Septuagint. The Greek version of the Hebrew Scriptures that dates from the third century BC.

Sitz im leben. Situation in life.

Sui generis. Being the only example of its kind; unique.

Swiss Reformers. John Calvin (1509–64); Philip Melanchthon (1497–1560); Ulrich Zwingli (1484–1531).

Synoptic tradition. Relating to the first three gospels of the New Testament (Matthew, Mark, Luke), which share content, style, and order of events and which differ largely from John.

Textus Receptus. Officially received texts.

Traditions hypothesis. Hypothesis pertaining to the tradition of the canon.

Trope (pl. tropoi). A figurative or metaphorical use of a word or expression.

Typological interpretation. The use of Old Testament figures and events as models for New Testament figures and events.

Ur-evangelium hypothesis. Hypothesis regarding which Gospel was the original.

Use hypothesis. Hypothesis regarding which Gospel the writer used.

Vaticimium ex eventu. Prophecy after the fact.

Glossary

Source: Where not otherwise indicated, definitions taken from The Free Dictionary (www.thefreedictionary.com) with additions and edits by R. Harrisville and R. Lundell.

Bibliography

Nestle-Aland. *Novum Testamentum Graece*. Stuttgart: Deutsche Bibelgesellschaft, 2013.
Auerbach, Erich. *Mimesis*. Princeton: Princeton University Press, 1953.
Augsburg Confession (CA XIV). In *The Book of Concord: The Confessions of the Evangelical Lutheran Church*, edited by Robert Kolb and Timothy J. Wengert, 27–106. Minneapolis: Fortress, 1993.
Austin, J. L. *How to Do Things with Words*. Cambridge: Harvard University Press, 1962.
Barth, Karl. *The Epistle to the Romans*. Translated by Edwyn C. Hoskins. Oxford: Oxford University Press, 1968.
Bauer, W., W. F. Arndt, F. W. Gingrich, and F. W. Danker, eds. *A Greek-English Lexicon of the New Testament and Other Early Christian Literature*. Chicago: University of Chicago Press, 2000.
Bayer, Oswald. *Martin Luther's Theology: A Contemporary Interpretation*. Grand Rapids: Eerdmans, 2008.
Best, T. F. "The Sociological Analysis of the New Testament: Promise and Peril of a New Discipline." *Journal of Theology* 36 (1983) 181–94.
Blass, F., A. Debrunner, and R. Funk, eds. *A Greek Grammar of the New Testament and Other Early Christian Literature*. Chicago: University of Chicago Press, 1961.
Braaten, Carl. *History and Hermeneutics*. Eugene, OR: Wipf & Stock, 2016.
Bultmann, Rudolf. *Die Geschichte der Synoptischen Tradition*. Göttingen, Germany: Vandenhoeck & Ruprecht, 1970.
———. "The Problem of Hermeneutics: Is Exegesis without Presuppositions Possible?" In *New Testament and Mythology and Other Basic Writings*, edited and translated by Schubert M. Ogden, 69–94. London: SCM, 1985.
E. C. Colwell. "A Definite Rule for the Use of the Article in the Greek New Testament." *Journal of Biblical Literature* 52 (1933) 12–21.
Dilthey, Wilhelm. *Selected Writings*. Edited by H. P. Hickman. Cambridge: Cambridge University Press, 1976.

Bibliography

———. *19 Jahrhundert: Positivismus, Historismus, Hermeneutik*. Edited by Manfred Riedel. Geschichte der Philosophie in Text und Darstellung 7. Stuttgart: Philipp Reclam, 1981.

Eagleton, Terry. *Literary Theory: An Introduction*. Minneapolis: University of Minnesota Press, 2008.

Fish, Stanley. *Is There a Text in This Class? The Authority of Interpretive Communities*. Cambridge: Harvard University Press, 1980.

Frör, Kurt. *Biblische Hermeneutik zur Schriftauslegung in Predigt und Unterricht*. Munich: Chr. Kaiser Verlag, 1961.

Frye, Northrop. *Anatomy of Criticism*. Princeton: Princeton University Press, 1990.

Gadamer, H. G. *Truth and Method*. New York: Bloomsbury, 2013.

Harrisville, Roy A. *Pandora's Box Opened: An Examination and Defense of Historical Critical Method and Its Master Practitioners*. Grand Rapids: Eerdmans, 2014.

Kittel, G., G.W. Bromiley, and G. Friedrich, eds. *Theological Dictionary of the New Testament*. Grand Rapids: Eerdmans, 1964–76.

Lewis, C. S. *An Experiment in Criticism*. Cambridge: Cambridge University Press, 2012.

Liddell, H. G., and R. Scott, eds. *A Greek-English Lexicon*. Oxford: Clarendon, 1983.

"Louise Rosenblatt." Wikipedia, n.d. https://en.wikipedia.org/wiki/Louise_Rosenblatt.

Louw, J. P., and E. A. Nida. *Greek-English lexicon of the New Testament: Based on Semantic Domains*. New York: United Bible Societies, 1988.

Luther, Martin. "To the Councilmen of All Cities in Germany that They Establish and Maintain Christian Schools." In vol. X of *Luther's Works*, 458–85. St. Louis, MO: Concordia, 2016.

Moore, Stephen D. *Poststructuralism and the New Testament*. Minneapolis: Fortress, 1999.

Moulton, W. F., and A. S. Geden. *A Concordance to the Greek Testament*. Edinburgh: T&T Clark, 1963.

Rahlfs, Alfred, and Robert Hanhart, eds. *Septuaginta*. Stuttgart: Deutsche Bibelgesellschaft, 2006.

Russell, Letty M., ed. *Feminist Interpretation of the Bible*. Philadelphia: Westminster, 1985.

Saldarini, A. J. *Pharisees, Scribes and Sadducees in Palestinian Society: A Sociological Approach*. Grand Rapids: Eerdmans, 2001.

Schakel, Peter J. *Imagination and the Arts in C. S. Lewis: Journeying to Narnia and Other Worlds*. Grand Rapids: Eerdmans, 2005.

Steiner, George. *Real Presences*. Chicago: University of Chicago Press, 1991.

———. *After Babel*. Oxford: Oxford University Press, 1975.

Stuhlmacher, Peter. *Historical Criticism and Theological Interpretation of Scripture*. Eugene, OR: Wipf & Stock, 2003.

Bibliography

Soden, H. *Norum Testamentum Graece cum apparatu critico curavit*. Berlin: Verlag der Weidmannschen Buchhandlung, 1930.

Thompkins, Jane. *Reader-Response Criticism: From Formalism to Post-Structuralism*. Edited by J. Thompkins. Johns Hopkins, 1980.

Tischendorf, C. von. *Novum Testamentum Graece: Editio Octava Critica Maijor*. Lipsiae: J. C. Hinrichs, 1884.

Tyson, Lois. *Critical Theory Today: A User-Friendly Guide*. New York: Routledge, 2014.

Von Rad, Gerhard. *Old Testament Theology*. Vol. 2. Translated by D. M. G. Stalker. Louisville: Westminster John Knox, 1965.

Westcott, B. F., and F. J. A. Hort. *The New Testament in the Original Greek*. New York: MacMillan, 1928.

Index of Authors

Aland, Barbara, 21
Aland, Kurt, 21
Alexandria, Clement of, 9
Alexandria, Cyril of, 10
Alexandria, Hesychius of, 20
Alexandria, Origen of, 9, 25
Aquinas, Thomas, 11
Aristotle, 11
Arminius, Jacobus, 14

Barr, James, 46
Barth, Karl, 15, 84
Bauer, Ferdinand Christian, 15
Beecher, Catherine, 75
Beecher, Lyman, 75
Bengel, Johann Albrecht, 18
Best, T.F., 55
Bonaventura, 11
Brown, Antoinette, 77
Bultmann, Rudolf, 15, 32

Calvin, John, 13
Chemnitz, Martin, 14
Chrysostom, John, 10, 25
Coleridge, Samuel Taylor, 70
Cremer, Hermann, 46, 47
Cyrus, Theodoret of, 25

Derrida, Jacques, 67
Dibelius, Martin, 15
Dilthey, William, 3

Epiphanes, Antiochus, 48

Erasmus, Desiderius, 12, 18
Ernesti, Johann August, 14
Estienne, Robert, 20

Fiorenza, Elizabeth, 76, 77
Fish, Stanley, 73
Flacius, Matthias, 14
Foucault, Michel, 68
Freud, Sigmund, 63

Gerhard, Johann, 14
Gieseler, Johann Karl Ludwig 28
Great, Albert the, 11
Griesbach, J.J., 28
Grimke, Sarah, 75
Grotius, Hugo, 14
Gunkel, Hermann, 15
Gutenberg, Johannes, 22

Hamann, Johann Georg, 61
Herder, Johann Gottfried, 28

Johnson, Barbara, 76
Josephus, Flavius, 52

Kant, Immanuel, 61
Kittel, Gerhard, 47

Lacan, Jacques, 68
Lessing, Gottfried Ephraim, 28
Lewis, Clive Staples, 70, 73
Lohmeyer, Ernst, 15
Luther, Martin, 4, 12

Index of Authors

Marx, Karl, 63
Melanchthon, Philip, 13
Michaelis, Johann David, 15
Michaelis, D.F., 28
Milan, Ambrose of, 10
Moore, Stephen D., 75
Mopsuestia, Theodor of, 10

Nestle, Eberhard Erwin, 21

Oeclampadius, Johannes, 13
Osiander, 13

Rad, Gerhard von, 5
Reimarus, Hermann Samuel, 15
Reuther, Rosemary, 76
Richards, Ivor A., 70
Ritschl, Albrecht, 15
Rosenblatt, Louise, 70, 73
Russell, Letty, 76

Saldarini, Anthony J., 55
Samosata, Lucien of, 10
Saussure, Ferdinand, 67

Schakel, Peter, 70
Schleiermacher, Friedrich D.E. 28
Schweitzer, Albert, 15
Semler, Johann Salomo, 14
Sinope, Marcion of, 9, 24
Stanton, Elizabeth Cady, 75
Steiner, George, 61
Strauss, Claude Levi, 63
Stridon, Jerome of, 10

Tischendorff, Constantin von, 18
Tompkins, Jane, 74
Trible, Phyllis, 76
Turretin, Francois, 14

Vitringa, Campegius, 14
Vorster, Willem S., 72

Wetstein, Johann Jakob, 14
Wettstein, Johan Jakob, 18
Wrede, William, 15

Zwingli, Ulrich, 13

Index of Scripture

OLD TESTAMENT

Proverbs

38

Isaiah

6:12	77
61:5–7	78

Daniel

9:27	48
11:31	48
12:11	48

NEW TESTAMENT

Matthew

2	72
3	72
5:3	54
5:3–11	57
5:6	54
5:39–42	29
5:44	29
5:45	29
5:46	29
5:48	29
6:6	54
6:27	35
6	29, 72
7:1	29
7:3–5	29
7:16–21	29
7:24–27	29
8:9	54
9:9	54
10:16	35
10:11	35
10:34–36	35
12:34	35
13:12	31
13:52	54
14–18	72
15	72
20	72
23	72
24:3–29	72
24:4–50	72
24:15	48
25:29	31
26	72

Mark

1:24–25	44
1:27	44
1:34	44
2:1–12	34
2:23–28	34
2:5	34
2:7	44

Index of Scripture

Mark (continued)

2:10	44
2:24–26	8
3:1–6	34
3:11–12	44
3:21	44
3:23	8
4:12	43
5:37	44
6:45–8:26	39
8:27–9:1	39
8:30	44
9:19	43
9:30	44
10:46	34
13	48
13:24–26	44
14:61–62	44
16:06	44

Luke

1:1–4	29
1:46–55	37
1:58–69	37
4:21	78
4:25–27	78
6:20	54
6:20–23	29
6:27–30	29
6:32–36	29
6:35	54
6:37	29
6:41–49	29
8:17	31
9	31
10	31
10:26	xi
12:02	31

John

1:1	78
1:1–18	38
4:4–26	68
7:23	78
7:37–39	78
10:35	7

Romans

1:3	37
1:13	37
1:15	38
1:29–30	38
3:25	37
4:25	37
5:1	24
5:3–5	58
5:5	25
5:9–11	25
5:15	59
5:17	59
6	38
6:1–29	59
6:12–14	59
7:5	38
9:19	58
10:9	37
12:24	59
13:13–14	38

I Corinthians

1:8–31	58
5:14	60
7:10	4
9:4–6	60
11:23	4
15:1	36
15:3	4
15:3–5	1

II Corinthians

3:10–11	8
3:14	9
6:4–10	57

Index of Scripture

Galatians
1:13–14	60
3:28	77

Colossians
1:15–20	38

I Thessalonians
2:3–10	48

II Thessalonians
2	48

I Timothy
3:16	38

Philemon
2:6–11	38
3:6	60

Hebrews
2:06	7
11:32	58

I Peter
1:20–21	7
3:5–6	59

Revelation
13:18	48

APOCRYPHA

Jesus Sirach
	38

1 Maccabees
1:54	48
6:7	48
59	48

www.ingramcontent.com/pod-product-compliance
Lightning Source LLC
Chambersburg PA
CBHW070929160426
43193CB00011B/1626